Praise f
Identity The

"Identity theft is everyone's opponent, but just like in basketball, the harder you prepare, the better your chances of winning. Steve Weisman shows you what you need to do in order to protect you and your family from identity theft."

John Calipari, head basketball coach, University of Kentucky

"There are people out there determined to wreck your life by stealing your identity. Nobody better prepares you to fight back than Steve Weisman. His new book, *Identity Theft Alert*, is why Steve's the guy I always turn to on this topic, on my 500 radio stations coast to coast. Steve should be the defensive coordinator of your identity, as well."

Jim Bohannon, nationally syndicated talk host, Dial Global Radio Networks

"Scammers, hackers, and thieves of all stripes should consider themselves warned. Steve Weisman is on to you and has armed the American people with knowledge, the most powerful tool of all. Comprehensive in scope, urgent in tone, *Identity Theft Alert* is a must-read for anyone concerned about identity theft...and that should be all of us."

Stan Rosenberg, Massachusetts State senator

"Identity theft has become the number one property crime in America today, and it can disrupt your life tremendously. What you don't know about identity theft can hurt you, but fortunately in this brilliant book Steve Weisman, a leading expert on identity theft, provides you with the tools you need to protect your identity."

Thom Hartmann, nationally and internationally syndicated radio and television talk show host; author of four *New York Times* bestsellers

"Steve's strength is staying ahead of the latest threats. Through his many guest appearances, he has provided my viewers with the information they need to prevent identify theft before it occurs. His new book puts his valuable knowledge all in one place and is a comprehensive plan for protecting yourself against identify theft."

Mike Nikitas, news and business anchor, NECN (New England Cable News)

"Steve Weisman's latest book, *Identity Theft Alert*, is essential reading for anybody who has a credit card, a credit history, a bank account; owns a phone; uses the Internet; or earns money for a living. Steve offers a sobering look at how scam artists operate. More importantly, the book offers practical advice on how best to protect yourself from these dangerous threats."

Mike Baxendale, co-host of the *Bax & O'Brien Show*, WAQY,
~~~~~~~~~~~~~~~usetts

IDENTITY THEFT ALERT

10 Rules You Must Follow to Protect Yourself from
America's #1 Crime

Steve Weisman

Associate Publisher: Amy Neidlinger
Operations Specialist: Jodi Kemper
Cover Designer: Chuti Prasertsith
Managing Editor: Kristy Hart
Senior Project Editor: Betsy Gratner
Copy Editor: Cheri Clark
Proofreader: Debbie Williams
Senior Indexer: Cheryl Lenser
Senior Compositor: Gloria Schurick
Manufacturing Buyer: Dan Uhrig

For information about buying this title in bulk quantities, or for special sales opportunities (which may include electronic versions; custom cover designs; and content particular to your business, training goals, marketing focus, or branding interests), please contact our corporate sales department at corpsales@pearsoned.com or (800) 382-3419.

For government sales inquiries, please contact governmentsales@pearsoned.com.

For questions about sales outside the U.S., please contact international@pearsoned.com.

Company and product names mentioned herein are the trademarks or registered trademarks of their respective owners.

Printed in the United States of America

First Printing July 2014

ISBN-10: 0-13-390252-8
ISBN-13: 978-0-13-390252-5

Pearson Education LTD.
Pearson Education Australia PTY, Limited
Pearson Education Singapore, Pte. Ltd.
Pearson Education Asia, Ltd.
Pearson Education Canada, Ltd.
Pearson Educación de Mexico, S.A. de C.V.
Pearson Education—Japan
Pearson Education Malaysia, Pte. Ltd.

Library of Congress Control Number: 2014939199

To Carole for yesterday, today,
and all our tomorrows

Contents

Acknowledgments

Many people have supported and encouraged my efforts in creating this book, and although I cannot name every one, I do want to mention a few.

Marc Padellaro, who teaches me more about everything every day and for whose friendship I am eternally grateful. He is a mensch above menschen.

Roger Weisman, who inspires me with his breadth of knowledge and insight.

Laurie Swett, my first and longest supporter, who really is as nice as people think she is.

Michael Harrison, my great friend and mentor.

Ron Nathan, a friend I can always count on.

Mark Peterman, Janice Peterman, and Laurie Priest of the peaceable kingdom, who help keep me centered.

Joe Newpol, Iris Berdrow, and Aaron Nurick, my colleagues at Bentley University who educate me as they do their students.

Saul Chadis, Peter Ettenberg, Marty Kenney, Bruce Newman, and Peter Seronick, whose friendship and support has stood the test of time—a long time.

Jennifer Sayles, my physical therapist, whose efforts enabled me to be able to type again. To quote John Mellencamp, "She hurts so good."

About the Author

Steve Weisman hosts the radio show *A Touch of Grey*, syndicated to 50+ stations nationwide, including AM 970 (NY) and KRLA (LA). A senior lecturer at Bentley University, he is a lawyer and is admitted to practice before the U.S. Supreme Court. He is also the legal editor of *Talkers Magazine* and a commentator on scams and identity theft for television station ABC 40 in Springfield, Massachusetts. He writes for publications ranging from the *Boston Globe* to *Playboy* and earned an ABA Certificate of Merit for excellence in legal journalism. His books include *The Truth About Avoiding Scams*, featured on Dr. Phil and CNN. Weisman holds a J.D. degree from Boston College Law School. He also operates the website www.scamicide.com, which provides the latest information on scams and identity theft.

Introduction

Identity theft is one of the most pervasive and insidious crimes of today, a crime that can tremendously disrupt your life—or even put you in jail for crimes you never committed.

This book explains the horrific details of the many identity theft scams that are so prevalent today. Story after story takes you into the dark world of identity theft and the dire consequences that can result from this crime that affects more and more people throughout the world. This book shows you just how vulnerable you are, but it also shows you steps you can take to protect yourself, as best you can, from becoming a victim. It also tells you what to do if you become an identity theft victim.

Identity theft is the biggest and fastest-growing crime in the world and with good reason. It is easy to perpetrate and easy to get away with.

No one is immune from identity theft—children, the elderly, and even the dead can have their identities stolen.

Through modern technology, an identity thief half way round the world can steal your identity from your computer, your laptop, your iPad, or your smartphone.

I can teach you how to recognize the risks of identity theft and how to avoid them.

What you don't know *can* hurt you. I will tell you how to spot dangers in places you might never have considered, such as your television, your cellphone, or even a copy machine.

In this age of information sharing, everyone is particularly vulnerable to identity theft because even if you are doing everything right, the many companies and institutions with which you do business and operate in your everyday life might not be protecting you as much as they can. I can show you how to minimize those risks.

This book might scare the hell out of you, and rightfully so. It explains just how vulnerable we all are in the world of identity theft. But it also tells you specifically what you can do to reduce your chances of becoming a victim and precisely what to do if you do become a victim of identity theft.

Many years ago, I worked as a professor in a college program in the state prison system in Massachusetts. One of my students was serving two consecutive life sentences, which meant that after he died, he would start his second sentence. When he told me about this, I told him how I had always wondered how that worked. He said that he had, too; when he was sentenced, he yelled at the judge, "How do you expect me to do two consecutive life sentences?" to which the judge responded, "Just do the best you can."

There are no guarantees in life and there certainly is no guarantee that you will not become a victim of identity theft; but by reading this book, you will learn how to do the best you can, and you can certainly narrow your chances of becoming a victim.

Bonus Online Content

You can access bonus content for this book at www.ftpress.com/identitytheft. There you'll find form letters and more information about the Gramm-Leach-Bliley Act, credit reports, identity theft insurance, identity theft and the elderly, and more.

1

Identity Theft

I dentity theft can result in your being hounded by debt collectors for debts you did not incur; becoming unable to access your own credit cards, bank accounts, or brokerage accounts; having your assets stolen; being arrested for crimes committed by people who have stolen your identity; or even receiving improper medical care because your medical identity has been stolen and your medical records have been corrupted. In addition, identity theft can ruin your credit rating, which can affect your chances to get a loan, get a job, get insurance, or rent a home.

Identity theft is the number-one consumer fraud in America, according to the Federal Trade Commission. According to a study by Javelin Strategy & Research, there were 12.6 million victims (which actually might be as many as 16.6 million victims) in 2013. According to the Justice Department's Bureau of Justice Statistics, the cost of identity theft to its victims in 2013 was $24.7 billion, which is $10 billion more than the cost of all other property crimes combined, and the crime is getting worse. As the global village becomes smaller and smaller due to the Internet, the conditions for international criminals committing identity theft from a world away have become greater. Unfortunately, as technology has continued to advance, legislative efforts to combat identity theft have not kept pace.

Terrorism and Identity Theft

Although the connection between terrorism and identity theft might not be immediately apparent, it is very real and threatening.

In his testimony of September 9, 2003, before the Senate Committee on Finance regarding the homeland security and terrorism threat from document fraud, identity theft, and Social Security number misuses, FBI acting Assistant Director of the Counterterrorism Division John S. Pitole said, "Advances in computer hardware and software, along with the growth of the Internet, have significantly increased the role that identity theft plays in crime. For example, the skill and time needed to produce high-quality counterfeit documents has been reduced to the point that nearly anyone can be an expert. Criminals and terrorists are now using the same multimedia software used by professional graphic artists. Today's software allows novices to easily manipulate images and fonts, allowing them to produce high-quality counterfeit documents. The tremendous growth of the Internet, the accessibility it provides to such an immense audience, coupled with the anonymity it allows, result in otherwise traditional fraud schemes becoming magnified when the Internet is utilized as part of the scheme. This is particularly true with identity theft–related crimes. Computer intrusions into the databases of credit card companies, financial institutions, online businesses, etc., to obtain credit card or other identification information for individuals have launched countless identity theft–related crimes.

"The methods used to finance terrorism range from highly sophisticated to the most basic. There is virtually no financing method that has not at some level been exploited by these groups. Identity theft is a key catalyst fueling many of these methods. For example, an Al Qaeda terrorist cell in Spain used stolen credit cards in fictitious sales scams and for numerous other purchases for the cell. They kept purchases below amounts where identification would be presented. They also used stolen telephone and credit cards for communications back to Pakistan, Afghanistan, Lebanon, etc. Extensive use of false passports and travel documents were used to open bank accounts where money for the mujahidin movement was sent to and from countries such as Pakistan, Afghanistan, etc."

When Al Qaeda leader Khalid Sheikh Mohammed, who was described in the 9/11 Commission Report as the "principal architect of the 9/11 attacks" on the United States, was captured in 2003, his laptop contained more than a thousand stolen credit card numbers.

According to a report on Identity Theft & Terrorism prepared by the Democratic Staff of the Homeland Security Committee in 2005, "Terrorists also steal identity information to gain access to credit or cash that can be used to finance their operations."

Who Are Identity Thieves?

Identity theft is an equal-opportunity crime. Identity theft is done by organized crime both in the United States and in foreign countries around the world, particularly Eastern Europe. Much of the rash of recent hackings of companies and government agencies in order to steal personal information to be used for identity theft purposes can be traced back to Russia. A 17-year-old Russian hacker, Sergey Taraspov, is thought to have written the computer program used to attack Target late in 2013. Taraspov is alleged to have sold the program on the black market for $2,000.

Although the name of Bulgarian Aleksi Kolarov is probably not familiar to you, it probably should be. In 2014 he was convicted of identity theft in federal court in New Jersey. For years, Kolarov was one of the leaders and operators of the website Shadowcrew.com, a black market website where stolen credit cards, debit cards, and bank account information were sold to the approximately 4,000 members of the criminal website. It has been estimated that Shadowcrew was responsible for the theft of 1.5 million credit cards, debit cards, and bank account numbers, resulting in fraud losses totaling millions of dollars to the banks issuing the cards.

According to the FBI, a Russian organized crime gang responsible for the data breach at Neiman Marcus in 2013 was also responsible for the theft of more than 160 million credit cards from numerous other retailers over the previous seven years.

Identity theft, however, is not solely the province of organized crime. It is done by small-time hoodlums, street gangs, your fellow workers, and even members of your own family.

What Do Identity Thieves Do?

Identity thieves take your personal information and use it to harm you in various ways, including these:

- Gaining access to your credit card accounts, bank accounts, or brokerage accounts
- Opening new credit card accounts in your name
- Opening new bank accounts in your name
- Buying cars and taking out car loans in your name
- Using your name and credit to pay for utilities, such as fuel oil or cable television
- Buying smartphones and phone plans in your name
- Using your medical insurance to obtain medical services, thereby corrupting your medical records
- Renting a home
- Using your name when committing crimes, for which you can be arrested

Although you might not be responsible for fraudulent charges made by an identity thief using your name, the damage to your credit as reflected in your credit report can affect your future employment, insurance applications, and loan applications, as well as future credit arrangements you might want to establish.

College Students and Identity Theft

College students are five times more likely to become victims of identity theft than the rest of the population, and they usually take longer to find out that they have been victimized. Living in close quarters and a lack of proper precautions are circumstances that make college students easy pickings for identity thieves.

TIP

Here is a list of things that college students should do to protect their identity:

- Lock computers, smartphones, and tablets when they are not in use
- Use a strong password and use different passwords for each device
- Use encryption software on all electronic devices
- Don't use Wi-Fi for financial transactions; it is too easy to infiltrate
- Because college mailboxes are not very secure, have sensitive mail sent home or sent to the student electronically
- Don't trust messages with links from "friends" that appear on the student's Facebook page
- Don't put too much personal information on Facebook pages; it can lead to identity theft
- Shred papers containing personal information before disposing of them
- Check bank statements and credit card statements carefully each month to look for signs of identity theft
- Get a free credit report from each of the three credit-reporting agencies annually

Malware and Macs

For many years, users of Apple computers have felt safe knowing that, by and large, most computer scams targeted users of PCs rather than Macs. However, with the increasing popularity of Apple computers and portable devices, more and more scammers and identity thieves have begun to tailor their illegal activities to Mac users. In the past, identity thieves often targeted their malware attacks against PCs because there were more PC users than Mac users. But now identity thieves and hackers focus much of their attention on Macs.

If you are a Mac user, you should have your computer checked for the presence of malware. Every computer user should have up-to-date security software that automatically updates and protects it from the latest malware and viruses.

Dumpster Diving

Dumpster diving is the name for the practice of going through trash for "goodies" such as credit card applications and other items considered to be junk by the person throwing out the material. In the hands of an identity thief, some of this trash can be transformed into gold in ways an early alchemist could never have imagined. Go to any post office and inevitably you will find in their trash containers much of this information that owners of post office boxes toss out when they go through their mail before they leave the post office. Too often people do not even bother to tear up the items. In the case of preapproved credit card offers, all the identity thief has to do is fill in the application, change the address, and send it back to the bank. In short order the thief will receive a credit card, and a careless individual will become the victim of identity theft as the identity thief begins to use the credit card and runs up debt in the victim's name.

You Are Only As Safe As the Places That Have Your Information

You will find that one of my recurring themes is that regardless of how careful you are about protecting your personal information from identity thieves, you are only as safe as the places that hold your personal information. These places include companies with which you do business, governmental agencies, and any club or association to which you belong. It is not unusual for rogue employees to steal the personal information of customers or members and either use it themselves for identity theft or sell the information to professional identity thieves. It is also important to note that small retail businesses have recently become a prime target for identity thieves because identity thieves have found that many of these businesses do not pay sufficient attention to maintaining the privacy and security of the personal data they hold.

So what can you do?

One thing you can do is try to limit as much as possible the personal information, particularly your Social Security number, that you provide to third parties. The Social Security number is a key element in identity theft. Armed with that number, an identity thief could find it a simple matter to steal your identity. Many establishments with which you do business routinely ask for your Social Security number even though they have no legitimate need for it. Recently, I was asked for my Social Security number when I went to my eye doctor. I responded by politely asking if it would be acceptable for me to provide my driver's license instead, and they were willing to accept that.

They Should Know Better

In recent years, large law firms have become a target of identity thieves because they have not instituted the proper data security measures necessary to protect the vast amounts of information they hold that, in the wrong hands, can lead to identity theft. As long ago as 2011, the FBI warned major law firms of the dangers of identity theft and corporate espionage, particularly law firms with foreign offices in China and Russia. However, not enough law firms have heeded these warnings, and many continue to put unencrypted information on thumb drives, e-mail unencrypted information to smartphones and iPads that are not secure, and use unsecured networks in countries such as China and Russia where hacking is rampant. Fortunately, many law firms are changing their practices under pressure from clients such as large banks who are threatening to withdraw their legal business unless proper security is initiated.

Hackers

Computer hacking of government and private business computers has resulted in the personal information of millions of people being compromised. Whereas at one time, the hacking of companies and businesses required considerable technological acumen, now cybercriminals need only go online to black market websites where they can purchase the necessary malware required to steal information from a targeted company or government agency. According to Trend Micro, a Japanese security software company, one particular type of hacking malware called BlackOS can be purchased on the black market for $3,800.

NO CURE FOR STUPID

According to comedian Ron White, "There is no cure for stupid." Far too often, owners of laptops or other portable electronic devices pave the way for identity thieves to gain access to personal information merely by stealing devices containing unencrypted personal information.

Identity Theft Risk in Old Gaming Consoles

Avid video game players are always excited about the release of the latest version of the popular consoles. Gamers who purchase the new gaming consoles generally sell their older gaming consoles on eBay or other sites after buying the newer version. To the surprise of many people, this can lead to identity theft. Video game consoles such as the Xbox and PlayStation are not just video game players, but also quite sophisticated computers that often have important personal information, including credit card information, stored on the computer's hard drive. Identity thieves know this and buy the used gaming consoles to harvest the personal information from the consoles and make their former console owners victims of identity theft.

If you are selling or otherwise disposing of your older video game consoles, make sure that you remove all personal information from the hard drives before you sell or get rid of them. The simplest way to do this is to get an external hard drive reader that you can use to connect your console's hard drive to your computer. After it is connected to your computer, you can use a program such as "Eraser," which is free, to remove your personal information from your console's hard drive.

The Drug Connection

Steven Massey was convicted of conspiracy to commit computer fraud and mail theft for his operation of an identity theft ring in which he enlisted methamphetamine addicts to plunder mailboxes and a recycling center for preapproved credit card applications and other material that could be used for identity theft. Methamphetamine addicts are perfectly suited for the crime of identity theft. They often stay awake for days at a time and can patiently perform boring tasks such as going through mail and even piecing together torn credit card solicitations. Drug money for identity theft information is a growing problem throughout the country.

TIP

When you are disposing of any papers or documentation that has personal information that, in the wrong hands, could be used to make you a victim of identity theft, it is important to first shred the documents before you dispose of them. However, you should remember to use a crosscut shredder rather than one that makes only vertical cuts because some identity thieves actually take the time to reconstruct documents that have been only vertically shredded.

Phishing

The term "phishing" goes back to the early days of America Online (AOL) when it charged its customers an hourly rate. Young Internet users with an addiction to their computers, not very much cash, and a bit of larceny in their hearts sent e-mails or instant messages through which they purported to be AOL customer service agents. In these phony e-mails, under those false pretenses, they would ask for their unwary victims' passwords in order to stay online on someone else's dime. After a while, this phony expedition, fishing for information, became known as "phishing."

Now, phishing is the name of the scam whereby you are lured to a phony website that appears to be legitimate, but when you click on links in these phony websites, download material from these websites, or provide information to these websites, you put yourself in danger of identity theft or of downloading dangerous keystroke-logging malware that can steal all the information on your computer including credit card numbers, your Social Security number, passwords, and various account information.

Federal Express Phishing Scam

Federal Express has often been the subject of phishing. Many of these phishing scams have come from the e-mail address of BillingOnline@fedex.com. These e-mails generally refer to a Federal Express invoice for which you are being billed. These are scam phishing e-mails, and if you enter personal information in order to dispute the bill, this information will be used to make you a victim of identity theft. You also might unwittingly download keystroke-logging malware that can steal the information from your computer and make you a victim of identity theft.

Federal Express does not send unsolicited e-mails requesting information regarding packages, invoices, account numbers, or personal information. If you receive such an e-mail, it is a scam. Do not open it and do not click on any links. If you have any questions as to the legitimacy of a Federal Express bill, contact them directly by phone or online at www.fedex.com.

Newegg Phishing Scam

Newegg.com is a legitimate company that sells computer and electronic products. Identity thieves have been sending phishing e-mails that look as though they have been sent by Newegg informing the recipient that his or her online sale has been completed and charged to his or her credit card. The notices look real, the logo looks accurate, and the bill doesn't have the grammatical mistakes found in many such scams. However, it is nothing more than a phishing scam. If you click on links within the e-mail in order to question the order, you will unwittingly download harmful malware onto your computer.

I actually received one of these scam phishing e-mails and took my own advice, which is whenever you have a question about the legitimacy of such an e-mail, call the company at a number that you know is accurate. So I called Newegg. Before I could even ask a question, a recording informed me that the invoice was a scam.

Former Good Advice

Smug consumers used to be able to identify a phishing expedition by merely looking at the Web browser's address window to determine whether the e-mail purporting to be from some company with which they generally dealt was legitimate. If the sender's e-mail address began with an unusual number configuration or had random letters, this indicated that it was phony. The e-mail addresses of legitimate companies are usually simple and direct. Unfortunately, this is not always the case. Now computer-savvy identity thieves are able to mimic the legitimate e-mail addresses of legitimate companies.

More Good Advice to Avoid Becoming a Victim of Phishing

Don't fall for the bait. It takes a few minutes longer, but if you are in any way inclined to respond to an e-mail that could be phishing to send you to a phony website do not click on the hyperlink in the e-mail that purports to send you directly to the company's website. Rather, type in what you know to be the proper website address for the company with which you are dealing.

As more people become aware of the dangers of phishing, identity thieves are adapting their tactics to use Internet search engines, such as Google or Bing, to lure people into clicking on links that people think will send them to a legitimate website, but that instead will download dangerous malware to their computers that can steal all the information on their computers and make them victims of identity theft. Identity thieves have been able to infiltrate search engines by adapting their phony websites that contain these dangerous links to be positioned on search engines to receive more traffic. People are less aware of this danger and are less skeptical of search-engine results than they are of e-mails with phony phishing links.

TIP

Many of the tainted websites are tied to celebrity news, such as videos of the latest Justin Bieber arrest or news of major world events that capture the public's interest. Identity thieves exploit the curiosity of the public with promises of tantalizing videos or stories. If you are searching for such information, you should limit your searches to websites that you know are legitimate. Because many of these search-engine phishing scams are based in Russia and China, you should be particularly wary of websites with links that end in .ru (Russia) or .cn (China). Both Google and Microsoft, which operates Bing, are acting to combat this type of scam, but it is a difficult task and you should not expect a solution soon.

The mysterious disappearance of Malaysian Airlines Flight 370 in 2014 captured the attention of people around the world, so it should come as no surprise that scammers and identity thieves promptly used this event as an opportunity to steal people's identity through malware-infected phony news reports, photos, and videos. In 2011 similar scams tied to the Japanese tsunami were common. Throughout the Internet and on social media, including Facebook and Twitter, following the disappearance of Malaysian Airlines Flight 370, links to phony stories, photos, and videos appeared with tantalizing headlines such as "Shocking video, Malaysian Airlines missing flight MH 370 found in Sea," "Malaysian Airlines missing flight MH 370 found in Sea—50 people alive saved," and "CNN UPDATE Breaking—Malaysian Airplane MH 370 Already Found. Shocking Video." Some phony links even promised videos of the plane in the Bermuda Triangle. Unfortunately, if you clicked on these links, all you succeeded in doing was unwittingly downloading keystroke-logging malware that could steal your personal information from your computer, laptop, tablet, or smartphone and use that information to make you a victim of identity theft.

The Dangers of Aquaman

Many people are fascinated by superheroes such as Superman, Green Lantern, and Batman. But you should always remember that whatever fascinates large numbers of the public also sparks the interest of identity thieves. These criminals set up phony websites and links on these websites that are traps for the unwary and can result in Internet surfers downloading keystroke-logging malware that can steal all the information from your computer and make you a victim of identity theft. Security software company McAfee released a list of the most dangerous superheroes of the Internet. Surprisingly, at the top of the list, with 18.60 percent of searches resulting in tainted websites, is DC superhero Aquaman, which is surprising because he doesn't even have a movie. Close behind Aquaman, at 18.22 percent, is Marvel Comics' Mr. Fantastic. The rest of the list in order is The Hulk, Wonder Woman, Daredevil, Iron Man, Superman, Thor, Green Lantern, Cyclops, Wolverine, Invisible Woman, Batman, Captain America, and last but not least your friendly neighborhood Spider Man, who, although having only 11.15 percent of tainted websites, still poses a significant risk to the unwary. Thus, Aquaman is even more dangerous than the most dangerous woman on the Internet, Emma Watson of Harry Potter fame. Internet searches of her will lead you to tainted websites loaded with viruses and malware 12.5 percent of the time. Also among the most dangerous women on the Internet are Eva Mendes, Halle Berry, Salma Hayek, and Sofia Vergara.

Iron Man 3

The movie *Iron Man 3* was a huge worldwide hit in 2013. Pirated versions of movies distributed on the Internet are a major problem for the movie industry, but they are also a major problem for consumers. I don't condone buying cheap bootlegs of movies over the Internet; that is a crime. However, I understand that many people will be tempted to purchase or even get free what they think are pirated versions of popular movies. Identity thieves understand this too, which is why soon after the release of *Iron Man 3* there were more than a hundred websites, not connected with the studio that produced *Iron Man 3*, claiming that they had copies of *Iron Man 3* for purchase or free in some instances. These sites required you to download a file containing a video player. The problem is that by downloading this video player, you might have downloaded keystroke-logging malware along with or instead of the promised video player. This malware can steal all of your personal information from your computer, including credit card numbers, bank account numbers, and passwords, and turn you into a victim of identity theft.

Nude Photos of Carla Bruni

The promise of nude photographs of Carla Bruni, the attractive wife of French President Nicolas Sarkozy, was used to phish into the computers of dozens of diplomats attending the 2011 Group of 20 economic summit. This group, generally referred to as the G20, is an organization of finance ministers and central bank governors from 20 major world economies. The ministers each received an e-mail with the subject line being "French first lady nude photos" and containing a link to connect to those photos. According to a French government source, almost all the ministers and bank governors receiving the e-mail took the bait and clicked on the link, which indeed did take them to nude photos of Carla Bruni. However, by clicking on the link, the ministers and bank governors also unwittingly downloaded keystroke-logging malware that was used to steal information from the computers of those hacked. It is worth noting that before becoming the wife of Nicolas Sarkozy, Carla Bruni was a model, actress, and singer who often posed nude, and her nude pictures can be readily accessed on the Internet without the viewer having to click on tainted links. The goal of the hackers from China who perpetrated this crime was most likely to obtain important financial information from these ministers and governors. The promise of nude photos being used to lure people into clicking on tainted links is nothing new. Every year this type of scam catches many unwary people.

Debit Card Phishing Scam

Customers of St. Anne's Credit Union, BankFive, Bristol County Savings Bank, Mechanics Cooperative Bank, Taunton Federal Credit Union, and Bridgewater Savings Bank in Massachusetts received telephone calls purportedly from their banks in which the caller told the person answering the call that the caller worked for his or her bank, that there was a security breach of the customer's bank account, and that the account had been frozen for security purposes. The customer was then told that in order to resolve the situation and make the account available to the customer again, the customer had to confirm his debit card number and PIN (personal identification number). Of course, the calls were not coming from the customers' banks. They were coming from identity thieves seeking this information in order to access the accounts of the people receiving the calls. In truth, not only were the calls not coming from the banks, but many of them came from identity thieves who were not even located in the United States.

TIP

Your real bank will not ask for your debit card number or PIN on the phone. Whenever you get a telephone call, text message, or e-mail requesting such information, you should refuse to provide it because you can never be sure that the communication is legitimate. In fact, in all circumstances, this will merely be a scam attempting to get your personal information in order to make you a victim of identity theft. If you have any thought that the communication might be legitimate, call your bank at a number that you know is legitimate to inquire as to the status of your account.

Another Debit Card Phishing Scam

Another debit card scam involves victims receiving text messages purportedly from their bank telling them that their debit card had been deactivated and to call a telephone number provided in the text message to straighten out the matter. Victims who fall for this ploy call the number and are instructed to provide their debit card numbers and PINs. What makes the identity thief's initial communication appear to be legitimate is that it often contains the first four digits of your debit card. However, the first four digits do not relate to you individually, but are associated with the particular financial institution and its location. This information is easy to get. It is also important to remember that financial institutions will never ask for your debit card number or PIN. They already have this information.

Phishing with a Large Net

The Phishing Attack Trends Report is published monthly online at www. antiphishing.org by the Anti-Phishing Working Group, an organization dedicated to eliminating identity theft resulting from phishing. A recent monthly report stated that the companies most often imitated by phony phishing websites were eBay, Citibank, AOL, and PayPal.

Phishing Around the World

In an effort to clean up their own house, EarthLink, the Internet access provider, went on a phishing expedition of their own, trying to trace the purveyors of phony phishing schemes, and what they found was both startling and disturbing. Many of the phishing scams they were able to track originated in e-mails from around the world, particularly Russia, Romania, other Eastern European countries, and Asia. In Romania, Dan Marius Stefan was convicted of stealing almost half a million dollars through a phishing scam and was sentenced to 30 months in prison.

For every computer geek or small-time phisher, such as convicted identity thief Helen Carr, who used phony e-mail messages purporting to be from AOL to steal people's money, it appears that more sophisticated organized crime phishing rings are popping up, posing a serious threat to computer and smartphone users. This presents a growing problem for law enforcement.

Spearphishing

Most often phishing e-mails are not directed at you by name, but rather to you as "customer" or "consumer." They also might appear to come from companies with which you do not do business, such as a bank where you have no accounts.

However, with the epidemic of hacking of large companies and governmental agencies, many identity thieves are able to use the hacked information to send you a personal, phony e-mail that contains your name and is definitely from a company or agency with which you do business, making you more likely to respond to the urging to click on the dangerous link contained in the e-mail. This type of targeted phishing is called "spearphishing" and it is extremely dangerous.

Never click on links in e-mails unless you are absolutely sure they are legitimate. If you get a link-containing e-mail from a company with which you do business, you should always be skeptical and make sure that you call the company before considering clicking on the link to confirm whether the e-mail is legitimate. The mere fact that the e-mail uses your name and even your account number does not necessarily mean that the e-mail is legitimate.

How Do You Know That You Have Become a Victim of Phishing?

The problem is that you might not know that you have been a victim of identity theft through phishing. When a mugger takes your wallet, immediately you know that your money has been stolen; however, when an identity thief steals your identity through phishing, you might not remember what appeared to be the innocuous e-mail, text message, or website that started you on the road to having your identity stolen. As always, an ounce of prevention is worth a gigabyte of cure.

Reloading

Reloading is the name for the scam when scammers go back to victims of scams, identity theft, or hacking, purporting to provide assistance in straightening out the mess created when the victim was first harmed, when in fact, what the scammers are actually doing is getting more money out of the victim under the guise of helping the victim or getting more personal information from the victim that leads to further identity theft. This happened in response to the Target hacking. Although Target was legitimately contacting its customers by e-mails, so were identity thieves purporting to be either Target or a consumer protection agency. In both cases, the identity thieves attempted to lure the victims into clicking on links in the e-mails. These links either downloaded malware onto the victim's computer and permitted the identity thief to steal all the information from the victim's computer and lead to the person becoming a further victim of identity theft, or led to a page where the victim was prompted to provide personal information directly, which would lead to identity theft. In other circumstances, the victim was told that he or she had to pay for assistance from the phony consumer protection agency.

No legitimate consumer protection agency such as the Federal Trade Commission or your local state attorney general's consumer protection division ever requires you to pay for their services. Never click on links in e-mails regardless of how legitimate the e-mails look until you have confirmed that they are indeed legitimate. In the case of Target, as with other companies, don't click on the links in their e-mails, but rather go directly to their legitimate website at an address that you know is accurate for further information. Also, do not provide personal information to anyone until you have confirmed that the person, company, or agency both is legitimate and has a real need for the information. Finally, make sure that your computer, laptop, tablet, and smartphone are all protected with the latest anti-malware software, and keep that software up-to-date.

Identity Theft Through Internet Phone Calls

Identity thieves have used unsolicited telephone calls in which they trick people into revealing personal information, such as credit card numbers or Social Security numbers, for many years. This has proven to be lucrative, but time-consuming. Now, however, some identity thieves are using modern technology such as automatic dialing software and Internet telephone services to make huge numbers of automated robocalls around the world in just a few moments. A typical scam using this technology involves a call purportedly from a person's credit card company telling him that his card needs to be reactivated and that the person receiving the call needs to punch in his credit card number. It is also important to note that some of these identity thieves also take advantage of a technique called "spoofing" by which the caller ID of the person receiving the call will appear to show a legitimate source for the call, such as the person's bank, when, in fact, the call is originating with an identity thief anywhere in the world.

It is easy to identify a scam robocall. All robocalls, with the exception of those from charities or politicians, are illegal, so if you receive one that indicates it is from your bank or a credit card company, it is a scam. In addition, when you receive a call, you can never be sure, regardless of what your caller ID might say, as to the identity of the person calling you; therefore, you should never provide personal information over the phone to anyone whom you have not called. If you do receive a call that appears to be legitimate requesting personal information, just hang up and call the real entity to find out whether the call was legitimate.

What Do Kim Kardashian and Michelle Obama Have in Common?

In 2013 Kim Kardashian, Kris Jenner, Ashton Kutcher, Paris Hilton, Joe Biden, Michelle Obama, Hillary Clinton, Bill Gates, Beyoncé, Mel Gibson, and FBI director Robert Mueller all became targets of identity theft, with Kris Jenner alone losing more than $70,000. Foreign hackers were able to steal the identities of 23 famous politicians, celebrities, and sports figures, including the aforementioned people, by hacking into the website www.annualcreditreport. com and getting access to their victims' credit reports. These reports provided a treasure-trove of personal information that, in the hands of an identity thief, could cause serious harm to the people whose information was stolen. Instead of quietly using this information as most identity thieves would do, these hackers publicized the information on the Internet, which is where identity thieves obtained this information and used it to steal from these victims.

Why this is important to you is that the initial hacker was able to get into his victims' credit reports due to a flaw in the authentication process at www. annualcreditreport.com. Without going into the details, the manner in which the security questions were set up made the system easy to crack, particularly when much of the information required to be furnished in order to answer the security questions and access the accounts could be found throughout the Internet. Certainly, public figures have much personal information available on the Internet for people to readily search out. You might think that you are not a public figure and that your personal information is not easily available, but think again. Too many people put too much personal information about themselves on social media, which then becomes fertile ground for someone trying to steal your identity. The lesson is that less is more. The less personal information you make available on social media, the more you protect yourself from identity thieves.

USB Sticks and Identity Theft

Curiosity killed the cat, and it can also invade your computer and result in an identity thief getting access to your computer through malware such as a keystroke-logging program that can read and steal all the information stored on your computer, such as your Social Security number, credit card numbers, and passwords. It can lead to your becoming a victim of identity theft. Identity thieves leave USB sticks in parking lots of companies that they want to hack, hoping that people who work there will see the USB sticks and then, being curious about what is on them, put them into their computers at work and unknowingly download the malicious software. Never put a USB stick that you are not absolutely sure is clean into your computer. The risk is too great. Let the cat live.

Internet of Things

As if we all didn't have enough to worry about, now we have the Internet of things about which to be concerned. More and more of the things we use are becoming connected to the Internet, including but certainly not limited to cars, refrigerators, coffee makers, and thermostats. It is tremendously convenient, for example, for us to use our smartphones to program our thermostats from afar so that our homes will have the proper temperature when we return from a day at work. But every technological advance, regardless of how constructive it might seem, has the potential to be exploited by scammers, hackers, and identity thieves. The Internet security company Proofpoint found that a botnet of more than 100,000 was made up of not only hacked computers but also (25 percent) Internet-connected devices including televisions and refrigerators. A botnet is a network of hacked electronic devices used by scammers and identity thieves to spread malware while avoiding detection.

The differences between computers and television sets have blurred in recent years, with many people buying Internet-connected high-definition televisions. Too often, people fail to recognize the security threats present in these new devices, much to their detriment. Hackers can breach your Internet-connected television and fool you into trusting phony bank or shopping websites, thereby making you a victim of identity theft. Fortunately, companies have developed security programs for Internet-connected television sets. Before you even consider buying an Internet-connected television set, you should make sure that you have it properly equipped with security software.

TIP

The danger posed by botnets of devices, part of the new Internet of things, is quite real and very chilling. Although many of us would not think of neglecting to provide proper security software for our computers, laptops, tablets, and smartphones, many people do not consider what they need to do to maintain the privacy and security of their refrigerator, car, and other devices that are a part of the new Internet of things. Unfortunately, among the people not giving enough attention to security in the Internet of things are the very companies developing these products. The most effective place to find a helping hand is at the end of your own arm, so whenever you are considering purchasing a convenient device with Internet capabilities, be sure to inquire as to the necessary security steps to take to make your use of the device safe.

What You Can Do to Prevent Identity Theft

As damaging as identity theft can be and as vulnerable as we are to identity theft, there are a number of relatively simple things you can do to make yourself less likely to become a victim of identity theft:

- Do a little spring cleaning in your wallet or purse even if it is the middle of summer. Do you really need to carry all the cards and identifications that you presently carry? In particular, don't carry your Social Security card in your wallet or purse. In the hands of an identity thief, it is the key to identity theft.

- If you rent a car while on vacation, remember to destroy your copy of the rental agreement after you have returned the car. Don't leave it in the glove compartment.

- Stolen mail is a ripe source of identity theft. When you are traveling, you might want to have a neighbor you trust pick up your mail every day or have your mail held at the post office until your return. Extremely careful people or extremely paranoid people, depending on your characterization of the same people, might prefer to use a post office box at the post office for receiving mail rather than a mailbox at home. Identity thieves also get your mail by filling out a "change of address" form using your name to divert your mail to them. If you find that you are not receiving any mail for a couple of days, it is worth contacting your local postmaster to make sure everything is okay. The U.S. Postal Service now requires post offices to send a "Move Validation Letter" to both the old and the new address whenever a change of address is filed. If you receive one of these notices and you have not recently changed your address, you should respond immediately because it could well be a warning that an identity thief has targeted you. A careful credit card user keeps an eye on his or her mailbox for the arrival each month of the monthly statement from the credit card company. If a bill is missing from your mail, it might mean that someone has hijacked your account and filed a change of address form with the credit card issuer to buy some more time. The sooner you are aware that the security of your account has been compromised, the better off you will be. You should also be particularly watchful of the mail when your card is close to expiration. An identity thief might be in a position to steal your mail containing your new card. If an identity thief is armed with enough personal information to activate the card, you could be in trouble.

- Prudent people might want to use travelers' checks while on vacation rather than taking their checkbook, because an enterprising identity thief who manages to get your checkbook can access your checking account and drain it.

- Be wary of who might be around you when you use an ATM (automated teller machine). Someone might be looking over your shoulder as you input your PIN. That same someone might lift your wallet shortly thereafter. Next step: disaster. In addition, ATMs are common targets for identity thieves who tamper with the machine by installing devices called skimmers that can read your card as you insert it into the machine. This information is then electronically transferred to the identity thief, who creates a duplicate of your card and is able to access your account. Never use an ATM if it appears in any way to have been tampered with, and always check for evidence of tampering in the slot where you insert your card. If it appears loose, go to another machine.

- Make copies of all of your credit cards, front and back, so that you can tell whether a card has been lost or stolen. Also keep a list of the customer service telephone numbers for each card. When copying your cards, you might also want to consider whether you really need that many cards.

- Be careful when storing personal information and mail, even in your own home. Louisiana police arrested a baby sitter on identity theft charges for stealing credit applications mailed to the people for whom she was baby sitting and for opening accounts using the Social Security number of her employer, which she obtained by rummaging through her employer's documents.

- After you have received a loan, a credit card, or anything else that required you to complete an application containing your Social Security number, request that your Social Security number be removed from the application kept on record. In addition, if you are feeling particularly paranoid (and it is important to remember that even paranoids have enemies), ask that your credit report used by the bank or other institution be shredded (cross shredded, remember?). They no longer need this information after you have received your loan. Holding your Social Security number in their data banks only serves to make you vulnerable to identity theft should the company suffer a data breach.

- Make life easier for yourself. Remove yourself from the marketing lists for preapproved credit cards and other solicitations. You can remove yourself from the Direct Marketing Association's solicitation list by writing to them at Mail Preference Service, Direct Marketing Association, P.O. Box 9008, Farmingdale, NY 11735. Include your name and address, but no other personal information. You can also take yourself off of the list of preapproved credit offers for five years by going online to www.optoutprescreen.com. Register for the Direct Marketing Association's Mail Preference Service to opt out of national mailing lists online at www.dmachoice.org. You can also print the form and get yourself removed from mailing lists. Additionally, at the same website, you can also remove yourself from commercial e-mail solicitations. When you go to www.dmachoice.org, go to the Consumer FAQ page, where you will find the links to remove yourself from these mailing lists. DMA members are required to remove people who have registered with the Mail Preference Service from their mailings. However, because the list is distributed only four times a year, it can take about three months from the time that your name has been entered to see a reduction in junk mail. It is also important to remember that many spammers are not members of the Direct Marketing Association, so you can still expect to receive some spam e-mails as well as spam snail mail.

- If you do get unwanted spam e-mails, do not click on the "remove me" link provided by many spam e-mails. All you will succeed in doing is letting them know that you are an active address and you will end up receiving even more unwanted e-mails.

- If you receive spam faxes, you also should be wary of contacting the telephone number provided in many spam faxes to remove yourself from their lists. It is already illegal for you to have received a spam fax. Contacting someone who is already ignoring the law by having sent you the spam fax might cost you for the call and will not reduce your spam faxes.

- Sign up for the National Do Not Call Registry to reduce unwanted telemarketing calls. Most telemarketers are legitimate. Almost all are annoying and many are criminals setting you up for identity theft or other scams. To sign up for the Do Not Call Registry, you may call toll free 888-382-1222 or register online at www.donotcall.gov. Again it is important to remember that criminals pay little attention to the Do Not Call Registry, so it does not prevent identity thieves and scam artists from calling you. However, knowing that a telemarketer calling you is in violation of the Do Not Call Registry is a good indication that the caller is not worth listening to and you should hang up right away.

- Check your credit report at least annually, and remember to get copies from each of the three major credit-reporting bureaus, all of which independently compile the information contained in their files. Federal law permits you to annually obtain a free copy of your credit report from each of the three major credit-reporting agencies: Equifax, TransUnion, and Experian. You can get your free credit reports by going to www.annualcreditreport.com or by calling 877-322-8228. It is important to note that there are a lot of companies that appear to be offering free credit reports, but if you read the fine print (and rarely will you find anything fine in fine print), you might learn that when you sign up for your "free" credit report with one of these companies, you will have also signed up for a costly monthly service that you might not have desired. A good indication that the offer to provide you with a free credit report is not "free" is when you are required to provide them with a credit card. Why would you need to provide a credit card number for a free service? The only official website from which you can truly obtain your credit reports free without any conditions is www.annualcreditreport.com. Be wary of websites with deceptively similar URLs. You also might want to consider staggering the obtaining of your credit reports by ordering one of your credit reports from each of the three major credit-reporting agencies every four months so that the information you are receiving is more current. Look over your file and make sure everything is in order. Particularly look for unauthorized and inaccurate charges or accounts. Also, check out the section of your report that deals with inquiries. A large number of inquiries that you have not authorized could be the tracks of an identity thief trying to open accounts in your name. A large number of inquiries can also have the harmful effect of lowering your credit score.

- Check your Social Security statement as provided by the Social Security Administration annually. It provides an estimate of your Social Security benefits and your contributions and can be helpful in detecting fraud. It is also a good thing to check this statement carefully each year to make sure that the information contained within it is accurate to ensure that you are slated to receive all the Social Security benefits to which you are entitled.

- Don't carry your Social Security card with you. You don't need it with you at all times, and if your wallet or purse containing your Social Security card is lost or stolen, you have handed over the key to identity theft to a criminal.

- Carefully examine your monthly bank and credit card statements for any discrepancies. This can be particularly important in limiting liability for the use of a stolen debit card.

- Carefully examine all medical bills and statements for services that you receive to make sure that medical charges are not being made for services received by someone else using your medical insurance.

- Never give personal information on the phone to someone you have not called. You can never be sure of the real identity of anyone who calls you. Even if you have caller ID and it seems to indicate that the call is legitimate, such as appearing to come from your bank, it might not be legitimate. Identity thieves are able to "spoof" legitimate numbers so that the number that appears on your caller ID appears legitimate when, in fact, it is not the real number calling you. If you believe that the call might be legitimate, merely hang up and call the company back at a number that you are sure is the correct and legitimate number.

- Protect your computer with a strong password as well as a proper firewall and with antivirus and anti-malware security software, and make sure that it is automatically updated.

- Protect your smartphone and other portable devices with security software and complex passwords.

- Shred, shred, shred any documents that you intend to discard that contain any personal information. Make sure that you use a cross shredder because vertically shredded material can be reconstructed by identity thieves. Although the IRS has up to six years in which to audit your income tax return if they allege you underreported your income by at least 25 percent, you are probably safe shredding income tax returns and supporting records after three years, the normal period for the IRS to perform an audit. Credit card statements, canceled checks, and bank statements should be shredded after three years.

- When doing any financial transactions on your computer, laptop, smartphone, or other electronic device, make sure that your communications are encrypted. This is particularly important if you are using public Wi-Fi.

- Don't share your passwords with anyone. Trust me, you can't trust anyone. Make sure that you use complicated passwords that are not something easily identified with you, such as your pet's name.

- Limit the information you share on social networking sites in order to make it more difficult for identity thieves to access personal information that can be used to make you a victim of identity theft.

- I know it is boring, but read the privacy policies of any websites you use where you provide personal information. Make sure you know what they do with your personal information, whether they share it with anyone, and how they protect it. What you read might surprise you and it might influence you to avoid that particular website.

- Not all of your personal information is on your computer and not all identity thieves come from Nigeria. Sometimes they are relatives, neighbors, or anyone else who might have access to your home and access to your personal records that might contain your Social Security number or other important personal information. Keep your personal and financial information documents locked and secure at home.

2

Making Yourself Less Vulnerable to Identity Theft

I dentity thieves believe that they deserve a lot of credit. Unfortunately, the credit to which they are convinced they are entitled is yours. Credit cards present an all-too-easy target for identity thieves. Protecting your credit cards from identity theft should be a priority for everyone. Take the following actions to reduce your chances of becoming a victim of credit card fraud:

- Sign your credit card as soon as you receive it and activate it. Some people believe that instead of signing your credit card, you should write "See ID" on the signature line on the back of the card. The hope is that whenever your card is used, the clerk or whoever is processing your purchase will check your ID to make sure that you are the one using your credit card. It sounds like a good idea, but credit card issuers are in general agreement that it is best to sign your card. Under the rules enforced between merchants and the major credit card issuers, Visa, MasterCard, and American Express, a merchant is supposed to compare the signature on the sales slip with the signature on the credit card. The merchant should refuse to go through with the transaction if the cardholder refuses to sign his or her card.

- As much as possible, do not let your credit card out of your sight when you make a purchase. A significant amount of credit card fraud occurs when the salesperson with whom you are dealing, out of your view, swipes your card through a small apparatus called a "skimmer" that gathers all the information embedded on the magnetic strip on your card. The thief then uses that information to make charges to your account. Skimmers can also be unobtrusively installed on ATMs, gas pumps, and any other machine through which you swipe your card. Always check any ATM or other machine for tampering before inserting your card.

- Save your receipts and ultimately destroy those receipts by shredding.

- Never give credit card information over the phone to anyone unless you have initiated the call.

Online Shopping Credit Card Protection

The opportunities for identity theft during online shopping are magnified. Two ways of reducing the odds are either through the use of a single-use card number provided to you by your card issuer or by the establishment of a password to be used when your credit card is used online.

The single-use authorization number is tied to your credit card, but has a distinct one-time-only effectiveness so that even if the number is compromised, your credit remains safe from identity theft.

Even less bothersome to a regular online shopper is the use of a password that you set up with your credit card issuer. When you enter your credit card number during an online purchase, a pop-up box will appear, requesting your password. After you enter the password, the transaction continues. As further security, the Internet retailer with which you are doing business never sees or has access to your password. So even if the retailer's security is breached, your credit card is safe.

More and more people are doing their online shopping on their smartphones and other portable devices. Unfortunately, many people are not vigilant in protecting the security of their smartphones and portable devices through proper updated security software, and identity thieves are well aware of this fact. One way that identity thieves get access to your smartphone is through corrupted free apps that you download that contain keystroke-logging malware that can read all the information contained in your smartphone or other device, including credit card numbers.

TIP

Download apps only from official app stores such as iTunes. Even then, read reviews before downloading them, and make sure that your smartphone and other personal electronic devices are properly protected with regularly updated security software.

Updated Web Browsers

Shopping online from your computer can be safe if you take the precautions to protect yourself from identity theft. Unfortunately, one of the most important aspects of safe shopping online is making sure that your Web browser is up-to-date, and recent studies have shown that 23 percent of people are not using the current version of their browser: 14.5 percent are using the previous version and 8.5 percent are using even older versions of their browsers. Browsers are so critically important because they are the software that your computer uses for e-mail, to connect with social media, and to surf the Internet. Identity thieves are constantly exploiting vulnerabilities in browsers, and browser manufacturers are just as constantly making adjustments to their products to close these vulnerabilities; however, their efforts are successful only if users download and install the updates.

SSL

SSL is the abbreviation for Secure Socket Layer, an Internet term for a protocol for transmitting documents over the Internet in an encrypted and secure fashion. Two-thirds of all websites use this technology. For years we all felt secure when we transacted business with a bank website or retail website because we knew that if the website used SSL, all of our communications were encrypted and protected from identity thieves. An indication that the website you are communicating with uses Open SSL is the presence of a tiny padlock icon next to the website address. Another indication that the website uses SSL is that at the start of the URL it reads "https" instead of "http." In April of 2014, we learned that this encryption technology had been cracked by attackers as long as two years earlier through a bug that came to be known as Heartbleed. This meant that we were wrong when we thought our communications online with banks, retailers, and others were safe. Fortunately, security patches were developed quickly upon learning of the security flaw, but everyone who had used any of the many websites involved was urged to change their compromised passwords. The lesson here is an important one: The Internet is always going to be a vulnerable place to be. No security technology is perfect and protecting your security is a full-time job.

DO NOT CALL

You might be like me and were thrilled to sign up for the national do-not-call registry to make your telephone off-limits to telemarketers. However, as an example of how everything is an opportunity for con men, a recent scam involves your being called by someone purporting to be from the National Do-Not-Call List who asks you to verify some personal information for the list. There is no reason why anyone operating a Do-Not-Call list needs any information from you other than your telephone number. Remember

Steve's Rule number one: Never give out personal information to anyone over the phone whom you have not called, and always be sure of to whom you are speaking.

CELLPHONE CAMERAS

Everyone uses the camera functions of their cellphones. They are easy to use. They are also easily and often used by identity thieves to photograph your credit card or your PIN as you input it; they then use the information gained to steal your identity. John Sileo, an identity theft and fraud expert, was on a business trip to Orlando, Florida, to give a speech to the Treasury Department about avoiding identity theft. He took the opportunity to take his daughter to Disney World while he was in Orlando. Upon returning to his hotel room after a day with his daughter at Disney World, he was informed by his bank that his credit card had been compromised and someone had stolen his identity and purchased $3,000 worth of goods online. It was determined that someone using a cellphone camera took a picture of Sileo's card when he used it at Disney World's electronic ticket booth.

A Primer on ATM Identity Theft

Bank robber Willie Sutton said he robbed banks because that was where the money was. That also explains the attraction to identity thieves of automated teller machines. ATMs offer an easy way to use identity theft to steal people's money. The plain, hard fact is that ATMs are vulnerable. There are many ways to steal money through an ATM.

Not all ATMs are owned by banks. Private individuals who are able to earn significant fees for ATM use by their customers own many ATMs. To set up a private ATM business, one needs an ATM, sufficient money to stock the machine, and a bank account into which the ATM card user's bank can send the funds necessary to reimburse the ATM-owning businessman for the money withdrawn and the use fee. There are absolutely no government regulations or licensing requirements. The banking industry itself sponsors independent service organizations that control the connecting of the privately owned machines to the bank networks. These independent service organizations, or ISOs, are intended to investigate and approve new private ATM owners, but the oversight is not particularly strong.

The owner of a privately owned ATM can install a mechanism within the machine that takes down and stores the account numbers and personal identification numbers of the people using the machine. The ATM-owning identity thief then just harvests the names, account numbers, and PINs and uses that information to steal money from the bank accounts of unwary victims.

Another scheme involves tampering with legitimate bank-owned and -operated ATMs by installing a thin, phony keypad over the real keypad. This phony keypad records PINs and enables identity thieves to obtain sensitive personal information without ever having to get at the inner workings of the ATM. The thieves just go back and retrieve their phony keypad whenever they think they have captured enough victims and then download the information. Then they are off to the races.

A third way that people have their identities stolen at ATMs is through the use of small hidden cameras that look over the shoulders of customers inputting their PINs. The cameras record the PINs and the identity thieves watch the whole transaction without having to be anywhere near the ATM.

IDENTITY THEFT AND THE ATM

If an identity thief fraudulently uses your ATM card or debit card, the federal Electronic Fund Transfer Act provides you with some protection. The amount of your protection, however, is significantly affected by how fast you notify the bank that you have been victimized. The maximum amount for which you can be held responsible for a stolen debit card is $50 if you notify the bank within two business days of learning that your card has been lost or stolen. If you delay notifying your bank more than two business days after discovering that your card has been lost or been used improperly, but within 60 days of receiving a bank statement showing that the card has been used for an unauthorized transaction, the maximum amount of your personal financial responsibility for the misuse of the card is $500. But if you wait more than 60 days after learning of the unauthorized use, you stand to lose everything that was taken from your account between the end of the 60-day period and the time that you reported your card was missing. It is best to notify your bank by telephone first and then immediately follow up your call with a written notification. It is important to note that both Visa and MasterCard have taken the consumer-friendly action of limiting their customers' liability for unauthorized debit card use to $50, regardless of the time it takes the customer to notify the bank.

Skimmers

Skimming is a growing problem and one that is going to get worse before it gets better. According to the U.S. Secret Service, thefts from ATM skimmers now total more than a billion dollars a year and this amount is expected to increase.

Skimmers are small plastic devices that fit over the slot where you insert your card into an ATM or another card-reading apparatus, such as is found on a gas pump. Often the skimmer takes the form of a thin plastic sheath over the slot where you insert your card. The skimmer reads the magnetic strip on the card as it is inserted and steals that information.

Dump Memory Grabber Malware

A new type of malware that is infecting credit card readers used at retail establishments as well as ATMs is posing a huge problem for American consumers using their credit cards and debit cards for purchases. The malware is called the Dump Memory Grabber malware. It is believed that the malware is the creation of Russian criminals. After it has been installed on a credit card reader such as you would commonly find at the checkout counter of many stores or an ATM, the malware is able to read the information encoded on the credit card or debit card, such as the name of the card holder, the account number, and the card's expiration date. This information is transmitted from the card reader or ATM to the criminal electronically. The information received is used to create fake credit cards that can be used to access the credit or, in the case of debit cards, the bank accounts of the people whose card information has been stolen. Credit and debit cards of Chase, Capital One, Citibank, and Union Bank of California are some of the banks that have been hit by this scam.

TIP

Unlike when a skimmer is used to steal someone's credit or debit card information, a person using an infected credit card reader or ATM has no way of knowing if the machine has been tampered with. The best thing you can do is to make sure that you constantly monitor your credit card bills for unauthorized purchases and report them immediately to your credit card issuer.

Federal Warning

In 2014, the Federal Financial Institutions Examination Council (FFIEC), a federal organization composed of representatives from various federal agencies dealing with financial matters such as the Office of the Comptroller of the Currency and the Consumer Financial Protection Bureau, issued a warning to banks about a wave of cyberattacks against ATMs. In particular, the FFIEC warned about a type of cyberattack it called Unlimited Operations, in which cybercriminals using phishing tactics managed to get bank employees to unwittingly download malware that took advantage of flaws in the bank's ATM software program, eliminating the ATM's limits on cash withdrawals and other security-related controls. The scammers then used counterfeit debit cards created with data obtained through the hacking of retailers and other methods to withdraw huge amounts of money from the attacked bank's ATMs. In one instance noted by the FFIEC, identity thieves were able to use this tactic to steal $40 million using only 12 debit cards.

Banks have not been as proactive as they should have been in protecting ATMs, as indicated by many successful ATM attacks. With 95 percent of the world's ATMs using the outdated Windows XP operating system as of April 8, 2014, the date after which Microsoft ceased to provide technical support and issue security updates for this software system, it can be expected that the attacks will worsen as vulnerabilities in the Windows XP operating system are exploited, as they were in the aforementioned $40 million cyberattack, until banks update to newer and more secure operating systems for their ATMs.

ATM Tips

ATMs are a great convenience, but they also present a significant risk of identity theft. Here are a few tips you should follow to prevent an ATM from turning into an identity thief's jackpot-paying slot machine:

- Avoid privately owned ATMs. Whenever possible, use ATMs of your own bank. This not only saves you from an increased danger of identity theft, but also lowers the fees you would otherwise pay for merely accessing your own bank account.
- Take a careful look at any ATM you are using for indications that its exterior has been tampered with.
- Look around for hidden cameras. Banks themselves will have cameras, but they are generally embedded in the ATM itself.
- If the keypad feels odd or if the keys offer unusual resistance to your touch, don't use it.
- When punching in your PIN, shield the keypad from any prying cameras or eyes that might be present.
- Give a little pull to the place where you insert your card into the ATM. If it is loose, it could be contaminated by a skimmer.
- Use ATMs inside bank buildings whenever possible because these are less likely to have skimmers installed.

Mailboxes

Most mailboxes come equipped with small red flags that when raised indicate that the owner of the mailbox has outgoing mail to be picked up by the mailman. They also can serve as an invitation to identity thieves to raid your mail.

An old-fashioned but still viable form of stolen mail identity theft occurs when your mail, containing checks to creditors such as credit card companies or your mortgage payment, is grabbed by an identity thief. The thief performs a process known as "check washing" through which the amount of the check is changed and the name of the payee is changed from the person or business to which you made out the check to the name of the identity thief. Common household cleaning products such as bleach can be used to "wash" the check and remove the name of the payee. The check is then rewritten payable to the identity thief in an amount of the thief's choosing.

In another more high-tech version of mailbox identity theft, the identity thief takes the check you are mailing and removes your check from the envelope to your credit card company, bank, or other payee and merely takes down the account numbers and bank routing numbers at the bottom of your check. Then, using easily obtained software, the thief creates perfect counterfeit checks that enable him or her to access your checking account.

In Woburn, Massachusetts, a newspaper delivery person stole $225,000 from his customers. He took the checks that he received as holiday tips from his customers and then, using the account information on the checks, counterfeited phony checks using perfectly legal check-creating software to create checks that enabled him to empty his victims' accounts.

And it is not just your outgoing mail that is fodder for identity thieves. Mail left in our mailbox by the mailman can include new credit cards. Social Security checks, income tax refunds, credit card applications, and credit card statements, as well as other documents, can be utilized for identity theft purposes. Stealing your incoming credit card bill will provide the identity thief with your credit card number, which can be used to access your account. Furthermore, an enterprising identity thief will also send the credit card company a change of address so that unless the victim is particularly vigilant, she might not notice that she has not received a credit card bill for a month or two, thereby providing the identity thief with more time to use the credit card with impunity.

In Oregon an identity thief stole checks from the back of a new checkbook that had been sent by mail to the account holder and delivered to the account holder's mailbox, from which the thief managed to steal the checks. He then merely forged the account holder's name on the real checks to draw money from the victim's account. Fortunately, the identity thief was at the bank cashing one of the stolen checks at the same time that the account holder was reporting the theft, and the identity thief was captured.

Not even the familiar blue legitimate United States Postal Services mailboxes you find on the corners of streets in every city and town are safe from identity thieves. In Indiana, law enforcement investigators uncovered an identity theft ring that utilized a combination of high-tech computers with a low-tech metal device that the identity thieves installed in the mailboxes. The device, which resembles a snorkel, is called a "mail stop." It collects the mail that later is gathered by the mail thieves without their having to make an apparent break-in to the mailbox, which would have alerted postal authorities. What the thieves looked for was the usual sensitive material, checks and billing account information, that could be transformed through sophisticated computer programs to produce counterfeit checks.

Mail Tips

The danger of identity theft is not limited to transactions done on your computer, smartphone, and other electronic devices. The use of regular "snail mail" carries significant danger of identity theft. Here are some tips to help you minimize the danger:

- When you are mailing checks, it is a good idea to mail them directly from the post office. Or better yet, try secure online bill paying. As for incoming mail, you might consider a locked mailbox or a post office box at the post office.

- If a credit card bill or bank statement is late in arriving, it might mean that your identity has been stolen and the identity thief has changed the address of the account. Always be vigilant in keeping track of the timely receipt of all financial account documents and bills.

- When ordering new checks, don't have them mailed to your home, where an identity thief can steal them from your mailbox. Pick them up yourself at your bank.

- When writing checks, use a special pen called a "gel ink pen." Gel ink is impervious to being removed from a check through check washing.

Denver Bronco Cheerleaders

Not long after Peyton Manning and the Denver Broncos lost the 2014 Super Bowl, it was their cheerleaders who took a hit. Law enforcement officials in Denver arrested two people who stole mail from mailboxes looking for checks, which they would then use to make counterfeit checks, which they would cash in order to access the accounts of the payers of the checks. Checks mailed by the Denver Broncos to their cheerleaders were stolen from the mailboxes of the cheerleaders, used to make counterfeit checks, and then cashed.

It is very easy to obtain a perfectly legal software program that will create legitimate checks, and this software can be misused to create counterfeit checks if the criminal has the bank information provided on actual checks of the companies whose checks they are counterfeiting. For this reason, if you are paying your bills by way of a written, paper check that you are mailing, you should never put it in your home mailbox and lift the red flag. Lifting the red flag might give notice to your letter carrier that you have outgoing mail, but it also gives notice to your friendly neighborhood identity thief that there is mail that might be useful for him to steal. Additionally, incoming mail with checks, credit card bills, or other information that can be used to make you a victim of identity theft is quite risky to have delivered to your mailbox unless you have a lock on your mailbox.

Identity Theft Threats on the Road

Both business and vacation travelers regularly use their smartphones and other personal electronic devices in airports, at hotels, in coffee shops, and at other public venues where unsecured wireless networks (Wi-Fi) can pose a threat if you do not have proper security software. Also, your smartphone security could be breached by an identity thief using Bluetooth. When you are in public, if you are not using your Bluetooth, turn it off.

> **TIP**
>
> When you are on the road, it is a good idea to encrypt sensitive information and not to input passwords or credit card numbers when using unsecured Wi-Fi. Also, when on the road be wary of using fax and copy machines to send or copy documents with personal information because these machines might store the information in a fashion available to identity thieves.

The FBI has warned the public about travelers connecting to the Internet in their hotel rooms using Wi-Fi having their computers infected with keystroke-logging malware when a pop-up appears notifying them of the necessity of updating commonly used software products. This occurs when the Wi-Fi is not actually the legitimate but unsecured Wi-Fi of the hotel, but rather a Wi-Fi set up by identity thieves in an adjoining room.

Hotel Wi-Fi

Identity theft victim Barbara Shaw knows all too well the dangers of hotel Wi-Fi. Upon returning to the United States from a European trip, she checked her airline frequent-flier account to make sure that she was credited with all the miles from her trip, only to find that more than 250,000 miles had been withdrawn from her account, converted into gift cards, and mailed to the identity thief who stole them from her account. Eventually, investigators discovered that Ms. Shaw had become a victim of identity theft while using what she thought was a hotel Wi-Fi system, when in fact it was a phony Wi-Fi system set up at the hotel at which she was staying. When she used the Wi-Fi at the hotel to go into her frequent-flier account, she provided the identity thieves all the information they needed to access her account.

TIP

Make sure that the Wi-Fi you are using is the legitimate Wi-Fi of the hotel, restaurant, or other venue that you are using. Confirm with the hotel or restaurant that the address of the Wi-Fi is the correct one. Any computer or tablet that has wireless capabilities activated should also have security software. One of the best ways to protect yourself when using Wi-Fi is to encrypt your data. Make sure that your wireless router has an encryption mechanism and that it is turned on. Even wireless routers that have encryption capabilities are often delivered with this feature turned off. It is up to you to make sure that your encryption feature is functioning. Most wireless routers also have a feature called identifier broadcaster that announces your presence to other devices in the Wi-Fi area. Make sure that yours is turned off so that you are not alerting anyone to your computer's presence. You also might want to consider using a Virtual Private Network (VPN). A VPN will encrypt your communications and route them to a server controlled by the VPN company so that if someone is eavesdropping on you through a compromised Wi-Fi, all they will have access to is encrypted data, which is worthless to them. Finally, even if your identifier broadcaster is turned off, wireless routers come equipped with a standard default identifier for your particular computer. This default identifier is known by identity thieves and hackers, so change your identifier so that your computer cannot be accessed by identity thieves and hackers.

More Hotel Tips

Staying in a hotel on vacation can be an extremely pleasurable experience. A vacation my wife and I recently took at the Grand Del Mar in San Diego was one of the most memorable vacations we ever had. Unfortunately, some people's vacations are memorable because they become victims of identity theft at their hotel. Vacationers at hotels are a frequent target of identity thieves. Here are some tips to keep your vacation from becoming memorable for all the wrong reasons:

- Make sure that your laptop or tablet has been updated with all necessary software changes before you go on vacation or a business trip. If while using the Wi-Fi at your hotel, a restaurant, or any other public place you are prompted to update your software through the unsecured Wi-Fi, do not click on the links provided through the pop-up; rather, go directly to the particular software vendor's official website to see whether indeed you need to update, and make any necessary updates directly from the vendor's safe website.

- Another common scam encountered by travelers is a telephone call to your room late at night from someone saying that he or she is the desk clerk and there is a problem with your credit card and that they need you to provide the number again to them over the phone. Never give personal information of any kind to anyone whom you have not called and of whose identity you are not absolutely sure. If you receive such a call at your hotel, it is most likely from an identity thief. If you have any question, tell the caller that you will come down to the front desk in the morning, or you can call the real front desk and see whether an issue does exist.

- Identity thieves are also finding hungry travelers a good target. Often identity thieves will put false advertising fliers for restaurant delivery services under hotel-room doors. When the unsuspecting travelers call the telephone number to order, they are asked for their credit card number, which too often they give, not realizing that they have been scammed until no food arrives. Confirm any food fliers with the hotel desk clerk to make sure you do not become a hungry victim of identity theft.

Identity Theft When Giving to Charities

It has often been said that no good deed goes unpunished, and certainly giving to charities is an example of how your good intentions can result in identity theft. Of course, there is always the risk that you are giving to a phony charity. A good place to check out whether a charity is legitimate is the website www. charitynavigator.org, which not only will tell you whether a charity is phony, but also will inform you as to how much of the charity's funds go toward its charitable purposes and how much toward administrative costs and salaries.

However, there is another place where even if you give to a legitimate charity, you could be at risk. Most charities are required to file a federal tax Form 990 (Return of Organization Exempt from Income Tax). This form provides much information from the particular charity. A five-year study by the group Identity Finder found that almost 20 percent of all nonprofit organizations required to file Form 990s included the Social Security numbers of charitable donors, scholarship recipients, tax preparers, employees, and trustees on these forms, which are totally available to anyone in the public. The worst part of this is that the law does not even require the inclusion of Social Security numbers on Form 990s. In response to this study, the IRS issued a warning to charities not to include Social Security numbers on Form 990s.

When making a charitable gift, never disclose your Social Security number to the charity. They don't need it and you don't need them to have it.

Job Scams

Many people search online for jobs through a number of legitimate websites, including Monster.com. Unfortunately, although Monster.com and many other companies try to monitor their job postings for legitimacy, they do not and cannot guarantee that identity thieves will not be there.

Never include your Social Security number or too much identifying personal information on your resume. Often identity thieves will request personal information, saying that it is for a routine background check. Never provide such information until you have checked out the company to make sure that it is legitimate and that the person contacting you allegedly representing the company is legitimate. Legitimate companies might do a background check on prospective employees, and to do that effectively, they will need your Social Security number. If you get to that point in the process, call the HR department of the company at a telephone number that you know is accurate to confirm that indeed the job offer is a legitimate one and not just an identity thief posing as that company. Identity thieves might ask for your bank account number in order to make a direct deposit of your salary. Again, don't give this information to a potential employer until you have confirmed not only that the company itself is legitimate, but also that you are not dealing with an identity thief who says he is with a legitimate company. A quick call to the legitimate company's HR department can provide the information you need to make a good decision.

Danger Where You Never Would Expect It

Most copy machines are complex pieces of machinery that since 2002 have contained hard drives that permit scanning, storing of documents, and other high-technology functions. Unfortunately, when you make a copy on such a machine, whatever you have copied remains on the hard drive, so if you were to copy an income tax return on a public copy machine, your personal information would be stored on the computer's hard drive, available to enterprising identity thieves who buy used copy machines. When the Federal Trade

Commission became aware of this problem, it notified copy machine manufacturers, and since 2007 all copy machines have been equipped with technology that either encrypts the data on the hard drive or provides for its erasure. Unfortunately, for copy machines manufactured between 2002 and 2007, this problem still exists.

TIP

Check the date of any copy machine you might use, and if it predates 2007, do not use it for copying documents that can make you a victim of identity theft. The easiest way to check on the date of the copy machine is to look at the instruction manual.

Shredding

As I have indicated previously, it is always a good idea to shred any documents containing personal information before discarding them. Identity thieves love to find their treasure in your trash if you have not properly shredded your important papers before throwing them away.

The annual Macy's Thanksgiving Day parade in New York City is a much anticipated event both by people who attend the event and by those watching on television. In 2012, however, there was another group of people who thoroughly enjoyed the parade: identity thieves. Mixed among the regular confetti showered down upon New York City were horizontally shredded documents of the Nassau County Police Department. Contained and visible in these shredded documents, even after shredding, were incident records that identified undercover police officers, names, phone numbers, addresses, Social Security numbers, and bank account numbers. The Nassau County Police Department had been considering using crosscut shredders instead of horizontal shredders, but had not done so at the time of the parade. The information contained in the records dumped on the city put many people in serious jeopardy of identity theft.

TIP

You are only as secure as the least secure place that holds your personal information, and when, as here, your personal information is literally dumped on the public, you are in serious danger of identity theft. The lesson here is twofold. First, all public agencies should use crosscut shredders, which will effectively render the shredded records useless to an identity thief. Many instances of identity theft can be traced back to dumpster diving by identity thieves who go through the trash of public agencies that do not properly shred their documents. The second lesson is to all of us as individuals. We should all be using crosscut shredders. Horizontal- or vertical-cut shredders just do not provide proper security. Keep your trash from becoming an identity thief's treasure.

More Steps to Take to Protect Yourself from Identity Theft

The bad news is that you can't do anything to guarantee that you will not become the victim of identity theft. The good news is that there are a number of simple (and not-so-simple) steps you can take that can reduce your chances of becoming an identity theft victim. Some seem a bit excessive and perhaps they are, but the decision is up to you. Remember, even paranoids have enemies.

- Consider paying bills online. It can be cheaper and more secure. But be sure that the online service you are using has security protection. Anytime you provide personal information online, make sure that the site is secure by confirming that the URL begins with "https" instead of merely "http." That extra "s" means that your data is being encrypted.

- Check your bank statements, telephone statements, credit card statements, and brokerage account statements regularly for unauthorized charges. Each month, when you get your statements, scrutinize them carefully to make sure that every charge is legitimate. Keep your statements in a safe and secure place. Use a shredder with cross-shredding capabilities to shred the statements when you no longer need them. If a monthly bill does not arrive on time, promptly notify the company. Sometimes a thief will use your personal information to get your credit card company or other company with which you do business to send your bill to a new address. In this way, the identity thief is able to prolong the period that he or she is able to fraudulently use your account before you or the company becomes aware of its improper use.

- Your mother was right. Don't talk to strangers. Updating Mom's advice, don't talk to strangers online. Do not download files that are sent to you from people you do not know. Your computer could be damaged through a virus or malware that permits an identity thief to access your personal information on your computer, tablet, laptop, or other device.

- Get a crosscut shredder to destroy all your unnecessary financial records as well as preapproved credit card offers. A horizontal shredder is not sufficient. Dumpster-diving identity thieves go through trash to find the mother lode of personal information that they transform into stealing your identity.

- Do not write down your PINs or passwords. However, be sure that whatever PIN or password you choose is not something that is easily associated with you, such as your name or your pet's name.

- Do not store your personal information on your laptop. Laptops have proven to be a tantalizing target for identity thieves. Many people prepare their income tax returns on their computers, forgetting about the sensitive information that might be left on their hard drives. Always remove this information from your computer upon completion of your tax return and keep a copy on a flash drive that you keep in a secure place.

- Get a good antivirus program and anti-malware program and keep them constantly updated. Viruses and malware can infect your computer without your being aware and might cause your computer to send information stored on your computer to the hacker that can be used to make you a victim of identity theft.

- Set up a firewall on your computer. A firewall is a computer program that makes it more difficult, but not impossible, for hackers to access your computer by preventing or selectively blocking access to your computer through the Internet. There are many free firewall programs that are easy to install.

- When you get rid of your computer, it is not enough to merely delete personal information. Deleted information remains on your hard drive and can be readily accessed by a computer-savvy identity thief. Make sure you use one of the special programs, such as the free program Eraser, that will effectively remove the information from your hard drive. Alternatively, you can do what I prefer to do, which is remove the hard disk from the computer and smash it into oblivion with a hammer.

- Put a credit freeze on your credit report at each of the three credit-reporting agencies. Through a credit freeze you are able to prevent access by anyone to your credit report even if they have your Social Security number. You are the only one who has access to your credit report by way of a PIN that you pick. If you need to apply for credit, you can temporarily lift the freeze on your credit report and then put it back when the company you want to have access to your report has finished.

- If you are in the military and are deployed away from home, you can place an active duty alert on your credit reports at each of the credit-reporting agencies that lasts for a year and can be renewed if necessary. This will restrict access to your credit report without your approval.

3

Danger on Your Computer and What to Do If You Are a Victim of Identity Theft

I t is hard to remember what life was like without computers, smartphones, tablets and other electronic devices. Imagine life without Candy Crush. E-mail, online shopping, and surfing the Net are only three of the uses of electronic devices that we take for granted in our everyday lives. But as much as computers and smartphones have enriched our lives, they have also made us much more vulnerable to identity theft. The first step in reducing your vulnerability to identity theft through your computer and other electronic devices is learning where you are vulnerable. However, assessing your risk is not enough. Unfortunately, there is nothing you can do to guarantee that you will not become a victim of identity theft, so it is also important to know what to do if you become a victim of identity theft.

Spyware

Spyware is software that is used to gather and remove confidential information from your computer, laptop, smartphone or other electronic device without your knowledge. Spyware is used by identity thieves to steal information from your computer or other device; they then use that information to make you a victim of identity theft. To make things worse some forms of spyware such as keystroke-logging malware can be installed on your computer or other device from a remote location without the identity thief ever having personal access to your computer or other device. You might think that it would be difficult for ordinary, law-abiding people to find spyware, but it is not. It is used by employers monitoring employees' computer use and parents who monitor their children's computer use. It has been rumored that sometimes it is even used by a not-too-trusting spouse who wants to know what his or her spouse is doing online. In addition, some file-sharing programs also contain spyware. Sometimes this information is used merely to send you advertisements for products and services that might interest you. "Cookies" planted by the spyware can be used to monitor your Internet use. Although cookies invade your privacy, they might have no more insidious intention than to tailor advertising to your specific interests and you might have actually agreed to have the spyware installed on your computer when you went to a particular website and accepted that website's user agreement, which can be long and filled with fine print that hardly anyone reads. Unfortunately identity thieves looking to steal your identity and maybe your money also use spyware.

What Can You Do About Spyware?

Sir Isaac Newton's Third Law of Motion was that for every action, there is an equal and opposite reaction. This also seems to apply to modern computer use (or misuse). For every spyware program, there also are antispyware programs that can let you know if your computer has been infected by spyware. Interestingly enough, some spyware developers use antispyware software to test the effectiveness of their own spyware and to try to make it less vulnerable to detection.

Although much of the installation of spyware on your computer is done remotely, some spyware programs are physically installed on your computer, so it is important to be sure you trust whoever repairs and services your computer.

Another way to protect yourself is through the installation of software programs that record every software installation that occurs on your computer. If you use this software, you obviously want to keep it hidden so that someone attempting to physically install spyware on your computer would be unaware that they are actually being monitored.

Anti-malware programs also work against spyware and they provide good additional, if not total, protection.

You can also take advantage of your Web browser's ability to prevent or limit cookies by changing your preference to disable cookies. An easy place to go to learn how to disable cookies is http://privacy.getnetwise.org/browsing/tools/.

Finally, return to Sir Isaac Newton and add to his laws of motion the axiom, "If you can't beat them, join them." Because spyware permits all of your computer's activities to be recorded, one way of telling that your computer has been accessed by someone with spyware is to install your own spyware in order to determine what has been going on in your computer.

It's Not Always Good to Share

Forget what you learned in kindergarten; it is not always good to share. Through file sharing, you can share music, software, videos, and games over the Internet. It is simple to do. Unfortunately, clicking on tainted links and downloading attachments from e-mails, text messages, in social media, and on websites is the primary way that identity thieves lure people into unwittingly installing keystroke-logging malware on their devices that will steal all the personal information on their computers, laptop, smartphones, tablets, or other devices.

Botnets

A botnet is a web of infected computers used by identity thieves and scam artists (the only criminals we refer to as artists) to send out spam, viruses and malware. Unwittingly, you might even be a part of the problem. It has been estimated that as much as 25 percent of home computers have been compromised by botnets that occur when, unwittingly people download the malware and become part of the botnet. Often the malware is downloaded through clicking on a link or downloading an attachment from an e-mail, phishing website, or text message promising free music, games, videos, or other enticements.

In 2011, the Department of Justice with the assistance of Microsoft Corp. disabled a massive botnet that had infected as many as two million computers for as long as ten years. This particular botnet originated in Russia and has been estimated as having led to the theft of $100 million over the ten years this particular botnet was in existence.

TIP

Often people find out that they are part of a botnet when their friends start receiving spam or malware-infected e-mails from the e-mail address of the person whose computer has been taken over as a part of the botnet. It is for this reason, that whenever you receive an e-mail or text message from a friend that has a link or an attachment in it, do not click on the link or download the attachment until you have confirmed that your friend actually is the one sending you the link or download. That e-mail or text might, in reality, be coming from an identity thief who is counting on you trusting the source because it appears to be coming from someone you trust. However, remember my motto, "trust me, you can't trust anyone." Of course, even if you confirm that your friend truly is the one who sent you the link or attachment, he or she might unwittingly be passing on a link or attachment riddled with malware. It is important to not only protect your electronic devices with anti-malware software, but to keep them constantly updated with the latest updates and patches. Even then you are not fully protected, because the makers of anti-malware software are always a step behind the identity thieves who are constantly identifying and exploiting new vulnerabilities in the programs that we all use.

What to Do If Your E-mail Is Hacked and Taken Over by a Botnet

It is not uncommon for your e-mail account to be hacked and taken over by a botnet. If this does happen to you, it is important to act promptly to remedy the situation. Here are the steps to take if your e-mail is hacked:

1. Change your password on your e-mail account. If you use the same password for other accounts, you should change those as well.

2. Change your security question. I often suggest that people use a nonsensical security question because the information could not be guessed or gathered online. For instance, you might want the question to be "What is your favorite color?" with the answer being "seven."

3. Report the hacking to your e-mail provider.

4. Contact people on your e-mail list and tell them you have been hacked and not to click on links in e-mails that might appear to come from you.

5. Scan your computer thoroughly with the latest antivirus and anti-malware program. This is important because the hacker might have tried to install a keystroke-logging malware program that can steal all the information from your computer.

6. Review the account settings on your e-mail to make sure that your e-mail is not being forwarded somewhere.

7. Get a free copy of your credit report. You can get your free credit reports from www.annualcreditreport.com.

8. Consider putting a credit freeze on your credit report.

Celebrity Malware

Identity thieves are always current in pop culture and ready to take advantage of the public's curiosity to lure us into downloading malware, such as keystroke-logging malware. Celebrity deaths, in particular, have provided a rich vein of identity thefts when people receive e-mails, text messages, or posts on their Facebook pages purporting to provide new and sometimes salacious details regarding the deaths of celebrities, such as Michael Jackson, Amy Winehouse, Steve Jobs, Whitney Houston, Paul Walker, and Philip Seymour Hoffman in recent years.

Pornography and Identity Theft

One of the biggest threats of identity theft occurs when people unwittingly download keystroke-logging programs that can read all the information in their computers and use it to steal the identity of the victim. Often this occurs when people go to websites or respond to e-mails that promise free music, free games, or free pornography. A study done by Dr. Christopher Ahlers, a German therapist, found that about two-thirds of the 60 million people who access free-pornography websites each day do so at work, which puts the data in their employers' computers in danger of being hacked and used for identity theft. This is no idle threat. A few years ago free pornography was used as the lure to hack into the computers of a Florida police department that resulted in more than 300,000 people becoming victims of identity theft. Employers should follow the lead of the Department of Defense, which has issued a prohibition against workers accessing pornography on their computers at work. (Sure, that will work.) Companies should make sure that they educate their employees about the dangers of identity theft in attempting to access free pornography, music, or games. The risk of identity theft through "free" pornography looms just as large on home computers and portable devices, so it is important to avoid dangerous websites and maintain proper security software on all of your electronic devices.

Keeping the Family Computer Safe

Often it seems that the teenage and even younger members of your family know more about computers than the adults do; and maybe they do. However, unfortunately, they are also often less security conscious and more susceptible to downloading malware such as keystroke-logging programs. Often the malware comes when the kids download free music, games, or videos. Scammers and identity thieves are adept at luring people, particularly young people, into downloading these virus-laden software programs that can lead to identity theft.

Along with good firewalls and computer security software, which you should regularly update, you should also educate your children about the risks of viruses and malware in free music, games, and videos. However, perhaps the best protection for the adults in the family—who should be using the computer for online banking, which is safer than paying bills through the mail—is to have one computer reserved for the adults that they use for online banking, online purchases, and the storage of sensitive information, and another that they share with the kids. In this way, you can avoid the risks of the kids downloading damaging malware. Now we just need to educate the adults to avoid the free pornography that is loaded with malware.

Help You Just Don't Need

According to a survey by Google, 15 percent of malware can be traced back to phony pop-ups that tell you that your computer has been infected by a virus and that you need to download their software to remedy the problem by linking to their antivirus software. Sometimes these phony pop-ups just steal your money and provide you with no solution to a problem that you do not have. Other times they prompt you to provide personal information that is used to make you a victim of identity theft.

TIP

Close your browser if you get this kind of a pop-up; then go to the antivirus and anti-malware software you use and run a scan of your computer. This is also a good time to make sure that your antivirus and anti-malware software is current with the latest updates. It is always a good idea to use security software that provides for automatic updating.

Wi-Fi—A Convenience to Worry About

Advances in computer technology are great. Unfortunately, they also often bring with them opportunities for identity theft. Starbucks is a very successful company. One of the perks of being a Starbucks customer is that they provide wireless Internet access in their stores so that people can sit back, drink some expensive coffee, and search the Internet. The way wireless Internet service or Wi-Fi works is by sending Web pages over radio waves to computers that have wireless capabilities. It is easy for technologically sophisticated identity thieves to hack into the computers of customers who are using their laptops or tablets at wireless access points, referred to as Internet "hotspots." Savvy hackers can join the network and access the information within the computers or laptops of the users of the systems. Wi-Fi is everywhere today. It can be found in malls, bookstores, coffee shops, and even McDonald's restaurants. Securing your computer, laptop, or other electronic device from hackers while using Wi-Fi facilities is often not even thought about by many users of technology who are also often unlikely to keep their computer security, antivirus, and anti-malware software up-to-date.

TIP

Any computer, laptop, tablet, or other device that has wireless capabilities should also have security software installed. One of the best ways to protect yourself when using Wi-Fi is to encrypt your data. Make sure your wireless router has an encryption mechanism and that it is turned on. Even wireless routers that have encryption capabilities are often delivered with this feature turned off. It is up to you to make sure that your encryption feature is functioning. Most wireless routers also have a feature called identifier broadcaster that announces your presence to other devices within the Wi-Fi area. Make sure that yours is turned off so that you are not alerting anyone to your computer's or tablet's presence. Finally, even if your identifier broadcaster is turned off, wireless routers come equipped with a standard default identifier for your particular computer, laptop, or tablet. This default identifier is known by identity thieves and hackers, so change your identifier so that your device cannot be accessed by identity thieves and hackers. And while you are at it, change your wireless router's default password to your own, more complex password.

E-mail Dangers

Checking our e-mail the first thing in the morning is as common as a morning cup of coffee. In fact, although most people will have, at most, only a couple of cups of coffee throughout the day, most of us check our e-mail constantly. It is a way of life.

Unfortunately, too many of us are careless when it comes to protecting our security when using e-mail, thereby making us vulnerable to identity theft. Often the problem is the use of passwords that are too easy to guess.

Passwords

Inadequate passwords present a danger not just on your e-mail account, but on any account that you use that requires a password. Following a hacking incident involving the company RockYou.com, which makes software for use on social networking sites, a list of 32 million passwords became public and confirmed what many of us already thought was the case—that too many of us use passwords that are far too easy for an identity thief to guess. The most popular password is the far from difficult to guess "123456" followed closely by the almost as difficult to guess "12345." Other common and much too easy to guess passwords include the very creative (think sarcasm) "password," "password1," "letmein," "trustno1," "iloveyou," "abc123," "monkey," "shadow," "sunshine," "princess," and the seemingly complex password "qwerty," which might appear to be a complex password until you look at the top row of letters on your computer keyboard.

Identity thieves and hackers use computer programs to quickly guess huge numbers of passwords, and yours might just be too easy to guess. A hacker's tool known as John the Ripper is capable of cracking millions of passwords in a single second. If your password is a word that appears in the dictionary, you are toast. Your password will be discovered by a hacker using password-deciphering software in less time than it would take you to type in your password.

The best passwords use 14 characters or more and contain a mixture of capital letters, small letters, digits, and symbols. Also, it is important to use a different password for every website because if your password is stolen as in a data breach at a particular website, you will not be in danger at other websites.

But how do you come up with good passwords and different passwords that you can easily remember? Start with a shortened phrase, such as "Idn'tlkPaswrd," and then add words that describe the site you are on, so if you are using this for Amazon, your password could be "Idn'tlkPswrdAm," and then for good measure add some symbols like "*" to come up with a password like "Idn'tlkPswrdAm**." This is a complex password that is tough to crack and easy to remember.

Some people use password-protection software such as LastPass, SplashData, and AgileBits, and they have worked well for many people. However, I am still wary of these because they are a tempting target for hackers, and although there have not been any security breaches to date, I am not willing to take that risk.

Security Questions

Another source of problems with e-mail security is a security question that is too easy for an identity thief to guess. Security questions are helpful in protecting your e-mail from being hacked by an identity thief, but if the question is too easy to guess, you might have unwittingly handed the key to your e-mail account to an identity thief. Unfortunately, too many people put too much information about themselves online through social media, such as Facebook. This makes it easy for enterprising identity thieves to get access to your e-mail account by logging on to the account and then indicating that they have forgotten the password or want to change the password. In both instances, a security question is used by the e-mail provider to confirm that the person is the legitimate user of the account. David Kernell was convicted of stealing access to former Alaska Governor and vice-presidential candidate Sarah Palin's e-mail merely by answering her security question, which asked where she met her husband. A quick trip to Wikipedia provided the answer to the question, which was Wasilla High School, and it was a simple matter from there for Kernell to change Palin's password and take over her account. You might think that your personal information is not as readily available online as that of Sarah Palin; however, you might be surprised as to both how much personal information about yourself you have made available through social media and how much is otherwise available online.

TIP

An example of a good security question is "What is your favorite sports team?" with the answer being "seven." This has the advantage of being impossible to guess due to its total lack of logic, and yet it is so weird that you will remember the answer.

E-Cards

Electronic greeting cards have become very popular and with good reason. Even if you don't remember a birthday or if you delay sending a holiday card until the last minute, you can send an electronic greeting card, often free, and have it delivered immediately. Many electronic greeting cards are quite entertaining, combining animation and music. Unfortunately, you can always count on scam artists and identity thieves to try to spoil anything, and electronic greeting cards are no exception. The scam starts when you get a phony electronic greeting card that requires you to click on a link to read the card. If you click on one of these phony greeting cards, you will end up downloading a keystroke-logging malware program that will steal all the information from your computer, and you will end up becoming a victim of identity theft.

TIP

One of the first things to notice is who is indicated as the person sending the card. If it states that the card is being sent by "a friend" or "an admirer," you can be pretty sure that it is a phony card. However, even if the card uses the name of someone you know, it still is risky to open the card without confirming with an e-mail or a phone call that your friend actually did send you the card.

Typos

Typographical errors are common, but they also can be dangerous. This is because identity thieves have registered the domain names of common misspellings of popular websites, such as Walmart or Apple, in an effort to lure you to their own websites. These sites look like those of the legitimate companies you are seeking, but unfortunately, they trick you into providing personal information that can be used to make you a victim of identity theft or prompt you into downloading dangerous keystroke-logging malware that can steal your personal information from your computer.

The Company You Keep

Unfortunately, it is not enough to do all that you can to protect the data that, in the hands (or computer) of an identity thief, can lead to trouble for you because you are only as safe as the weakest security programs of the companies and agencies with which you do business.

We Regret to Inform You

A few years ago, GMAC notified 200,000 of its customers that their personal information might have been compromised (a euphemism for "possibly stolen") following the theft of two laptop computers used by GMAC employees that were stolen from an employee's car. Although the data stored on the particular laptop computers was protected by password-access technology, the data itself was not encrypted as a further prudent security measure. The data on the computer was extremely sensitive material including names, addresses, birth dates, and Social Security numbers of GMAC customers. This security breach is not uncommon in an era when employees might take work home on their laptops.

It is not even just the companies with which you do business that should concern you. It is also the companies with which they do business and with which they might share your personal information. The Bank of Rhode Island contacted 43,000 of its customers to warn them that their personal information, including Social Security numbers, might have been compromised. A laptop computer used by an employee of Fiserv, Inc., a company with which the Bank of Rhode Island did business, was stolen. The laptop contained sensitive personal information about Bank of Rhode Island customers.

California, a state that has often been the leader in identity protection laws, has had a law since 2003 that requires any business that has had a breach of its computer security to notify its customers. Similar laws have been passed in 45 other states, although there is little uniformity among these different state laws. This is one area where a comprehensive and consistent federal law is very much needed.

TIP

Ask any company with which you do business about their policy for the security and protection of your personal information, including whether your information is encrypted in their computers. If their answers do not satisfy you, take your business elsewhere.

Lures

Before the release in late 2012 of the Halo 4 Xbox video game, some identity thieves were circulating e-mails and websites promising free copies of the game before its official release. These were just phishing scams intended to lure gamers into downloading keystroke-logging malware that would lead to identity theft. Similar scams occur before the release of other new video games and the latest versions of technological devices.

Java Danger

Computer hackers are constantly exploiting vulnerabilities in software to attack your computer and steal information from it that can make you a victim of identity theft. The dirty little secret is that computer security software is not very effective against the newest viruses and malware. Studies have shown that it takes the software security companies about a month to catch up with the latest viruses. During that time you are extremely vulnerable to viruses and other malware despite having the latest security software on your computer. Java software made by Oracle has been a particularly successful target of hackers and identity thieves. According to Kaspersky Lab, flaws in Java software were responsible for about half of all the cyberattacks by hackers in recent years. Much of the recent wave of attacks by hackers against American companies by the hundreds involved Java software vulnerabilities. In early 2013 the Department of Homeland Security identified new and dangerous vulnerabilities in Java software that can lead to your identity being stolen and your computer being compromised by hackers. The Department of Homeland Security even went as far as to advise that people disable Java or prevent Java apps from running in their browsers.

TIP

I strongly advise people who do not need to use Java to disable it. Here is an important link from the Department of Homeland Security with information on how to disable Java or to otherwise deal with its vulnerabilities: www. us-cert.gov/ncas/alerts/TA13-064A.

Adobe

Adobe makes software used by millions of consumers. In the Fall of 2013, Adobe announced that it had been hacked and personal information belonging to 38 million of its customers was stolen. The stolen information included names, encrypted credit card numbers, and expiration dates, as well as information pertaining to individual orders.

The Adobe data breach occurred over a period of as much as five months before Adobe discovered the breach. It was not until a computer security company alerted the public to the hacking that Adobe itself made a public statement about it, even though 46 states have laws requiring companies to notify their customers of data breaches when they occur. The Adobe breach was much worse than many of the other major data breaches in recent years because hackers not only got information about customers, but also got source code for the Adobe Acrobat PDF reader and the Adobe ColdFusion Web app developer's tool. This enabled identity thieves and hackers to poison PDFs that you open on a tainted website such that when you use Adobe Acrobat to read the PDF, you unwittingly download malware such as keystroke-logging malware that could steal all the information from your computer and use it to make you a victim of identity theft. Adobe ColdFusion is used by many creators of mobile apps and websites, so when you use their apps or websites, you again download dangerous malware.

Adobe was targeted both because it is very popular and because it is very vulnerable. The codes for many of its programs are old and not state of the art. It is easier for hackers and identity thieves to find and exploit vulnerabilities in these programs. The Adobe ColdFusion program is used by many companies and governmental agencies in the construction of websites. Even the Department of Defense uses it. It is entirely possible that, in stealing the code, hackers would be able to steal databases from agencies and companies that use these programs. This is not a far-fetched idea. Earlier in 2013 the National White Collar Crime Center, which uses Adobe ColdFusion, had its data stolen in this manner. Consequently, anyone using Adobe products is potentially at risk because if you use their software or go to a tainted website, you might end up unwittingly downloading keystroke-logging malware. Even if you have up-to-date anti-malware software, you might still be vulnerable because the makers of anti-malware software are always at least a month behind in protecting against the latest viruses and malware.

TIP

Whether or not you were directly affected by the Adobe breach, you should consider using a PDF reader other than Adobe. There are many free ones available that are more secure than Adobe, such as Evince or Sumatra PDF. You can find a list of them at www.pdfreaders.org.

A Few Ounces of Protection—Protecting Yourself Online from Identity Theft

Merely because you are vulnerable to identity theft on your computer is no reason to avoid using your computer to access the Internet; however, some good protective measures can go a long way toward protecting yourself while online:

- Install good security software to protect your computer from viruses, spyware, and other malware. There are many legitimate companies that offer free security software; but make sure that you are dealing with a reputable company and consider paying for a product that will provide you with greater protection.

- Keep your security software up-to-date. Automatic updates are best.
- Encrypt the data on your laptop. Microsoft's BitLocker will do the job free. TrueCrypt is another free encryption service that will protect the data on your computer from prying eyes in public.
- Use strong, difficult-to-guess passwords.
- Never turn off your firewall. Firewalls maintain a protective barrier between your computer and the Internet.
- The price of computer security is eternal vigilance along with a healthy dose of mistrust. Never download anything from a source that you do not absolutely trust, and even if you trust the source—don't. First, communicate with the source to make sure that the material you are being asked to download or link to is actually from that person or company that you trust, and even then, remember that even if they weren't hacked and the material didn't come from someone who took over their e-mail account, your friend might unintentionally be sending you corrupted material.

A Pound of Cure—What to Do If You Are a Victim of Identity Theft

Don't feel too bad if, despite your best efforts, you become a victim of identity theft. You are in good company. The list of prominent victims includes Oprah Winfrey, Michael Jordan, Tiger Woods, Steven Spielberg, Ted Turner, Warren Buffet, former New York City Mayor Michael Bloomberg, Robert DeNiro, Martha Stewart, Will Smith, and Ross Perot. Fortunately, there are some steps you can take to respond to the theft of your identity and to minimize the damage:

- Put a fraud alert on your credit report. If you think that you might be the victim of identity theft, you can have a fraud alert placed on your credit report at the credit-reporting agencies. The alert stays on your credit report for up to 90 days, but can be extended for up to seven years. When a fraud alert has been put on your credit report, you are entitled to a second free credit report during that year in order to monitor your credit for further irregularities. In the past people placing a fraud alert on their credit reports found that for it to be effective, they had to call each of the three major credit-reporting agencies to have fraud alerts independently placed on each company's record. Now under FACTA (the Federal Fair and Accurate Credit Transactions Act), all you need to do is call one of the credit-reporting agencies and they are required by law to notify the other two to place the fraud alert on your file. Unfortunately, fraud alerts are not always as effective as you might think. The law does not require businesses to check for fraud alerts before granting credit, and there are no penalties for companies failing to monitor credit reports for fraud alerts. Many companies do not even bother to check for fraud alerts.

- A better solution might be to place a credit freeze on your credit report. This service, available in all states, permits you to effectively seal your credit report from access by anyone (such as an identity thief with your Social Security number and other personal information) without the use of a PIN that you pick to make your credit report available. Thus, an identity thief is prevented from using your credit report to secure credit or open a new account in your name. Consumers Union has a very user-friendly website that can help you access the credit-freeze law for your particular state at http://defendyourdollars.org/document/guide-to-security-freeze-protection. Even if you have not been a victim of identity theft, a credit freeze is a great preventive measure to take to protect yourself from identity theft.

- Go to the Federal Trade Commission's website at www.consumer.ftc.gov/articles/pdf-0094-identity-theft-affidavit.pdf to obtain the FTC's ID Theft Affidavit and use it to report the crime.

- Contact all your creditors by phone and then follow up with a letter sent by certified mail, return receipt requested. Get new credit cards with new account numbers. Change your PINs and your passwords.

- Close tainted accounts. When opening new accounts with these creditors, use a password that is not easily connected with you. A word to the wise: Do not use your mother's maiden name or, to be particularly safe, do not even use my mother's maiden name. People think that their mother's maiden name is difficult to find. It is not. It is on your birth certificate, a public record.

- When you close accounts, make sure that the accounts are designated as being closed at the customer's request due to identity theft so that when information is transmitted to the credit-reporting agencies, it is clear that the problems are not of your doing.

- Ask your creditors to notify each of the credit-reporting agencies to remove erroneous and fraudulent information from your file.

- If your checks are stolen, promptly notify your bank and have the account closed immediately. If your checking account is accessed by checks with forged signatures, you obviously have not authorized the withdrawals and should not be held responsible for money stolen from your account. However, if you neglect to monitor your account and fail to promptly notify your bank when there is an irregularity in your account or your checks are lost or stolen, you might be held partially responsible for your losses. It is not even necessary to have your checks physically stolen to become a victim. An identity thief armed with your name, checking account number, and bank routing information can use one of a number of inexpensive software programs to create checks for your account.

- Contact the various check-verification companies and ask that they in turn contact retailers who use their services, telling them not to accept checks from your accounts that have been accessed by identity thieves. Check-verification services are companies that maintain databases of bad check writers. Retailers using their services contact the verification service's database before accepting checks. Among the companies that do check verification are CellCharge, CheckCare, and CrossCheck.

- To see whether checking accounts have been opened in your name, contact ChexSystems at www.consumerdebit.com to request a free copy of a report that lists all checking accounts in your name. If you find that an account has been opened in your name, contact the bank and instruct them to close the account.

- File a report with the police both where the fraud occurred and where you live. You might find police departments reluctant to accept your report, sometimes for technical legal jurisdictional reasons. Remind them that credit bureaus will prevent fraudulent accounts from appearing on your credit report if you can provide a police report. Give the police officer taking the report as much documentation as you have to support your claim, including the ID Theft Affidavit approved by the Federal Trade Commission. When a police report has been filed, send a copy of it to each of the three major credit-reporting agencies.

- Be proactive. Contact your creditors where you have tainted accounts and get a written statement from each of them indicating that the account accessed by an identity thief has been closed and that the charges made to the accounts are fraudulent. Request that they initiate a fraud investigation. Find out what you are required to do to advance the investigation, such as providing them with a police report. A sample letter to your creditors requesting such a statement is included in the online content at www.ftpress.com/identitytheft. These letters can be very helpful, particularly if the credit-reporting agencies mistakenly resubmit the fraudulent charges on your credit report. Remember to get a written copy of your creditors' completed investigations.

- Send copies of your creditors' completed investigations to each of the three credit-reporting agencies. Ask them to send you a copy of your updated credit report in order to confirm that any erroneous and fraudulent information has been removed from your file.

- If fraudulent charges do appear on your credit report, notify the credit-reporting agencies in writing that you dispute the information and request that such information be removed from your file. See the bonus content at www.ftpress.com/identitytheft for a sample letter.

- If you are contacted by a debt collector attempting to collect a debt incurred by an identity thief in your name, write to the debt collector within 30 days of receiving the initial notice from the debt collector. Tell the debt collector that the debt is not yours and that you are a victim of identity theft. Send a copy of your identity theft report, police report, or other reports you might have completed. After you provide this information, the debt collector is required by law to cease collection efforts until they have verified the accuracy of the debt. Additionally, you should also contact the company for which the debt collector is attempting to collect the debt and explain to them that the debt is not yours, but rather is the result of identity theft. Also, ask them to provide you with details about the transaction creating the debt, including copies of documentation that might contain the signature of the identity thief. Finally, contact the credit-reporting agencies and ask that they block the incorrect information from appearing on your credit report.

- If your driver's license is possibly in the hands of an identity thief, you should cancel the license and get a new one.

- If your passport is lost or stolen, contact the State Department at http:// travel.state.gov/content/passports/english/passports/lost-stolen.html to arrange to get another passport and to have it recorded that your passport has been lost or stolen.

- If your mail has been stolen and used to make you a victim of identity theft, the Postal Service will investigate the crime. Notify the Postal Service at your local post office.

- If an identity thief has used your identity to set up phony accounts for utilities such as phone, cable, electricity, or water, contact the utility provider and report the crime. Provide them with a copy of your identity theft report and close the account. You should also contact your state public utility commissioner's office and inform them about the crime and provide them with your identity theft report so that they can investigate this as well.

- If your information has been used to obtain a student loan in your name, contact the school or the lender, provide them with the identity theft report, and ask them to close the loan. You should also report the crime to the Office of the Inspector General at www2.ed.gov/about/ offices/list/oig/hotline.html.

- If your Social Security number has been misappropriated by an identity thief, contact the Social Security Administration at www.socialsecurity. gov, or by phone on their fraud hotline at 800-269-0271, or by mail at Social Security Administration Fraud Hotline, P.O. Box 17785, Baltimore, MD 21235.

4

Your Social Security Number—An Identity Thief's Lucky Number

Allow an identity thief access to your Social Security number and in a very short time you will be victimized. Armed with your Social Security number, an identity thief can readily access your bank accounts and other assets, as well as establish credit and run up debts in your name. Protecting your Social Security number requires great diligence. When the Social Security Administration was created in 1936, the public was assured by the government that the use of the identifying numbers would be limited to Social Security programs. So much for government assurances. The Social Security number has become a national identifying number. It is used by the federal and state governments, businesses, banks, credit-reporting agencies, utility companies, universities, healthcare providers, insurance companies, and many more institutions. With the Social Security number the easiest tool for identity theft, your identity is only as secure as the security of the many places that keep a record of that number. Large-scale data breaches of companies keeping Social Security numbers in data banks place all of us in jeopardy. Some of these data breaches have gone on for years without being discovered.

Treasure-Trove of Social Security Numbers

The federal government's General Accountability Office estimated in 2006 that 85 percent of the counties within the United States had records available online that contained Social Security numbers. Some state and local governments are making an effort to change this, but for many older records, Social Security numbers can still easily be obtained despite the efforts of government to redact these numbers from older records.

Biggest Offender

One of the biggest offenders when it comes to misusing Social Security numbers is our own federal government through the Medicare program. Despite numerous studies and warnings of the dangers of doing so, Medicare still uses a person's Social Security number as the identifying number appearing on a Medicare recipient's identification card.

Social Security Identity Theft Threats in the Military

According to a study done by the Federal Trade Commission, members of the military are twice as likely to become a victim of identity theft. One of the primary reasons for this is the military personnel's Social Security number. Until recently, all military ID cards used the Social Security number, and although the Department of Defense has changed its policy and is now issuing military IDs with a unique Department of Defense number, the transition to these numbers started only in 2011 and will take four years to complete. Therefore, many members of the military still have the old ID cards. In addition, although Veteran Identification Cards no longer show the veteran's Social Security number on the card, the person's Social Security number is still embedded in the magnetic stripe on the back of the card, so identity thieves who, through various pretenses, manage to scan the card can obtain the Social Security number anyway. These cards are also being phased out, but many veterans still have them.

Members of the military with the old-style cards should be particularly careful about providing the card as identification and should limit its use as an identifier whenever possible. Members of the military are eligible for an Active Duty Alert to be placed on their files with the three major credit-reporting agencies that requires creditors to verify the identity of anyone before issuing credit in the name of the member of the military, but a credit freeze, which locks your credit report and requires a PIN to make it available, is probably a better choice.

Social Security Number Protection Act of 2010

This law prohibits all federal, state, and local government agencies from displaying a person's Social Security number on any check from the government. In a Congress that had difficulty agreeing on anything, this law passed unanimously in the Senate and passed the House of Representatives by a voice vote. Although it might seem like common sense to not put a person's Social Security number on a government check, at the time the bill was passed into law, many states and municipalities still did this dangerous practice that increased the risk of identity theft.

Another provision of the law banned the use of prisoners on work release or in any other capacity from doing work for any governmental entity in which the prisoners would have access to Social Security numbers. Again, this would seem like common sense, but apparently common sense is not particularly common, as facilities in eight states at the time of the enactment of this legislation used prison labor for work where prisoners would have access to records containing names and Social Security numbers.

The Good News and the Bad News

The good news is that you are not legally required to provide your Social Security number to most private companies that ask for it for identification purposes. The bad news, however, is that there are no federal laws that prevent businesses from asking for it, and they can refuse to do business with you if you do not provide it. Only Alaska, Kansas, Maine, New Mexico, New York, and Rhode Island restrict the requesting of Social Security numbers by providers of goods and services.

Unavoidable Social Security Number Disclosure

When obtaining a credit card, credit, or a loan of any kind, you will generally be required to provide your Social Security number both as verification of your identity and so that the grantor of credit can evaluate your creditworthiness by checking your credit report with one or more of the three major credit-reporting agencies: Equifax, TransUnion, and Experian.

A good way to avoid the annoying (at best) and identity-theft-risky (at worst) "preapproved" credit card offers is for you to call 888-567-8688 to have your name removed from the mailing lists used to generate these offers. Unfortunately, if you do so, you must provide your Social Security number when making the call. However, you also can have your name taken off of the list to receive preapproved credit card offers by going online to www. optoutprescreen.com, where providing your Social Security number is optional.

TIP

If you order an annual free copy of your credit report from each of the three credit-reporting agencies, as everyone should, you should request that your Social Security number be deleted from the copy, if you are going to have it mailed to you.

Doing Business Online

Some companies with which you do business online such as insurance companies might not do business with you unless you provide your Social Security number. Extra precautions are necessary anytime you provide your Social Security number through the Internet.

First, make sure that your firewall and security software are operating and fully up-to-date. Second, make sure that the website you are on is also doing its part in protecting your data through encryption. The simplest way to do this is to check the URL or web address at the top of your screen. If it starts with "http," it is not a secure site and you should not provide any personal information, particularly your Social Security number. If it reads "https," you can feel safe that the information you provide is being encrypted and protected.

Social Security Numbers and College Students

Although federal law generally prohibits the release of personally identifiable information of students by colleges and universities, which would include the Social Security numbers of college students, some colleges and universities do not interpret the law as prohibiting them from using Social Security numbers as student identification numbers on student ID cards or on class rosters or grade listings. Presently only Arkansas, Arizona, Colorado, New York, West Virginia, and Wisconsin have state laws that limit the use of Social Security numbers as student identification numbers.

TIP

If you are a student or the parent of a student whose school still uses Social Security numbers in this fashion, you can request an alternative number. Your chances of success will be enhanced if you argue that to fail to do so would violate 20 USC Section 1232, a federal law that provides for privacy rights in education.

My Social Security Account

The Social Security Administration permits you to set up your own online "My Social Security Account" with the SSA. You can use this account to obtain your benefit verification letter, check your benefit records, change your address, and start or change the direct deposit of your benefit payment.

The Inspector General for the Social Security Administration has issued a warning to the public to be aware of identity thieves who are stealing personal information from Social Security recipients and then setting up a "My Social Security Account" in the name of the identity theft victim online at the website of the Social Security Administration. The identity thief then uses the account to redirect the identity theft victim's Social Security check to a bank account controlled by the identity thief. If you are receiving Social Security benefits and have personally not set up a My Social Security Account online and you receive information from the Social Security Administration that such an account has been opened in your name, this is a red flag that you have become a victim of identity theft.

If you are presently receiving Social Security benefits and have not yet set up a My Social Security Account online with the Social Security Administration, I urge you to do so. This will not only protect you from an identity thief setting up an account in your name, but also provide you with quick access to much information and services related to Social Security.

Driver's License

In 1996, the Federal Immigration Reform Act made it mandatory for each of the states to obtain the Social Security number of every applicant for a driver's license in an effort to reduce illegal immigration. Unfortunately, a side effect of this legislation was that more states started using your Social Security number as your license number. Fortunately, in 2004 Congress passed the Intelligence Reform and Terrorism Prevention Act of 2004, which prohibited all the states from using your Social Security number as an identifying number on your driver's license or registration.

Many health insurance cards also use your Social Security number as the identifying number on the card. Request a new number.

The Federal Drivers Privacy Protection Act bans states from providing your personal information to marketers without your permission. Do not give this permission. It would only make you more vulnerable to identity theft. Although the law prevents the individual state departments of motor vehicles from providing your personal information to marketers, they are allowed to give this information to law enforcement agencies, courts, government agencies, insurance companies, and others with a legitimate need for this information.

When and Where Must You Provide Your Social Security Number?

There are a few scenarios in which you must provide your Social Security number, including income tax returns, medical records, credit reports, loan applications, and driver's license applications.

Restrictions on the Use of Social Security Numbers

Recognizing the threat of identity theft presented by the prominent display of Social Security numbers, the federal government has taken a number of steps to reduce their use. The IRS no longer puts Social Security numbers on the preprinted labels sent to taxpayers. The Social Security Administration itself ceased using Social Security numbers in written communications wherever possible, and the Treasury Department, since 2004, no longer includes Social Security numbers on Social Security checks. Unfortunately, Medicare cards continue to carry the Medicare recipient's name and Social Security number, thereby making Medicare-receiving senior citizens more susceptible to identity theft.

Workplace Identity Theft

Regardless of how vigilant you might be in your personal life in maintaining the privacy of your Social Security number, your job might put you in jeopardy of identity theft. Employers must have access to the Social Security numbers of their employees. Phony employers seeking your Social Security number for identity theft purposes present obvious problems. Less obvious, however, is the risk you face from the lax personal information security of some employers. Your employer's information security problems can easily become yours.

Looking for a Job

Although not typically thought of as a threatening situation, online job postings can be fodder for identity thieves. There are many legitimate online employment companies, but even they can be scammed and list phony job descriptions for the purpose of luring people into becoming victims of identity theft. Monster.com has specifically warned its users that false job postings are used to collect sensitive, personal information from unwary job applicants. With a few simple precautions, however, you should be able to avoid becoming an identity theft victim through an online job listing. One thing to remember is that there is no need to send a prospective employer any information that is obviously unrelated to your obtaining employment. No employer needs to know your bank account numbers or credit card numbers, and certainly not your mother's maiden name. The tough call is when an employer asks for your Social Security number because it is legitimate for an employer to look at your credit report for employment purposes. The best and most prudent course of action is to ask whether you can wait until a meeting in person with a prospective employer before providing that critical piece of information to anyone about whose legitimacy you have even the slightest concerns.

I Gave at the Office

Burglaries at the workplace are on the rise. And sometimes the thieves are not concerned with the money in your wallet. They want your identity. A purse left out in the open is fair game for the thief, who might grab a credit card, or even your driver's license, to aid in identity theft. This booty could be used by the thief directly or sold to another identity thief who just uses the services of such petty thieves. Be careful. Keep your purse or other personal information secured at all times. Employers should enact policies to restrict access to work areas by visitors and unauthorized persons unless authorized personnel accompany them.

Temporary Worker—Longtime Problem

With so many businesses having control of sensitive personal information today, it is imperative that businesses become much more cognizant of security measures to protect that information. An area of particular concern is temporary workers who might not be screened as carefully as full-time hired employees. In California, Anthony Johnson was convicted of obtaining personal information through his job as a temporary worker at an insurance company. He used the information to facilitate identity theft to the tune of $764,000, which is actually more of a symphony than a tune.

TIP

Employers working with a temporary-office-help agency should inquire as to the extent of the screening and background checks the agency performs on its employees. You also might want to limit the access of temporary workers to personal information in your records.

Preventing Identity Theft at Work

Protecting the security of information stored in computers at work from identity thieves is the responsibility of both employers and employees. Here are some tips to provide for a more secure workplace:

- Anyone who has access to your workspace might have access to your computer and the information contained therein. Fellow workers, visitors, business support personnel, or, at worst, burglars can get at the information in your computer unless you protect it. Use passwords for sensitive information. Turn off the computer when you are not using it, or set the computer to automatically log out after a few minutes of nonuse.

- Use encryption programs.

- Do not have your passwords stored in your software for frequently visited websites. Log them in each time you visit a site. You might want to change your password periodically. If you do, mix letters and numbers to make your password less vulnerable. And, of course, it is important to have passwords you can remember.

- When you replace your computer, make sure that the hard drive on your old computer has all the information stored there permanently erased. Merely deleting information on your computer does not permanently erase data. There are a number of inexpensive software programs that will permanently remove information from your hard drive.

Higher Education and Identity Theft

You would think that the best and brightest minds at our colleges and universities would be particularly cognizant of the problem of identity theft and the importance of using the latest technology to maintain the security of sensitive student data such as their Social Security numbers—but you would be wrong.

School of Thieves

It is taking too long for many institutions to realize that access to Social Security numbers is the first step toward someone becoming victimized by identity theft. Unfortunately too many colleges and universities still use Social Security numbers on student identification cards, registration for classes, class rosters, and postings of grades.

A Washington University philosophy professor (apparently not well versed in ethics, a basic philosophy course) was sent to prison for stealing the Social Security numbers of students and utilizing the numbers in a credit card fraud scheme.

Oops

An employee of the California State University at Monterey Bay mistakenly moved information on close to 3,000 applicants to a computer folder that was not secure. The employee unwittingly put this information out over the Internet, where it was seen more than 100 times before the mistake was caught and remedied.

Campus officials at New York University learned that a number of university mailing lists containing names, birth dates, addresses, telephone numbers, e-mail addresses, and even some Social Security numbers for more than 2,000 current students, alumni, and professors were mistakenly posted on an easily accessible campus website. A list of more than 11,000 MIT employees' Social Security numbers and MIT identification numbers was found to have been posted on the Internet for more than six months. It does not take a rocket scientist to realize that this is not a good thing. The information was accidentally placed on the Internet, but the threat of identity theft was just as real as if an identity thief had posted that personal information.

TIPS FOR PROTECTING YOUR SOCIAL SECURITY NUMBER

Here are some essential steps you can take to protect the privacy of your Social Security number:

- Don't carry your Social Security number with you in your wallet or purse. Keep it in a secure location.

- Even when asked for your Social Security number by a company or agency, ask whether they will accept an alternative identifying number, such as your driver's license. Many will understand and comply with your wishes.

- Don't write your Social Security number or have it printed on your checks, address labels, or any other circulated item.

- Make sure that you order your free copy of your credit report from each of the three major credit-reporting agencies each year at www.annualcreditreport.com. This will enable you to see whether your Social Security number has been compromised or whether there are any other Social Security numbers associated with you.

- As odd as it might seem, limit sharing your birthday, age, or place of birth online, particularly on social media. A study done at Carnegie Mellon University in 2009 found that to a significant degree a person's Social Security number can be guessed based on this information. The Social Security Administration for a long time assigned Social Security numbers partly based on geography. Particularly for people born since 1989 when Social Security numbers were assigned shortly after birth, it is relatively easy to predict a person's Social Security number. And it also makes it easier for an identity thief who knows the first five digits to trick a victim into providing the remaining digits through phishing or some other scheme. It also is easy for an identity thief to use botnets to send out thousands of applications for credit with various guesses at your Social Security number until he or she hits the right one.

Fortunately, since 2011 the Social Security Administration has been assigning Social Security numbers randomly. But for anyone reading this book, your Social Security number remains predictable and you should be aware of the risks.

5

Criminal Identity Theft, Taxes—And More Arresting Problems

I dentity theft can take on repercussions that you can hardly imagine. You can be arrested for a crime committed by someone who has stolen your identity. You can become an identity theft victim merely by filing your tax returns or what you think are your tax returns. You can have your tax refund stolen before it ever reaches you. You can even be sued by companies with which you do business seeking compensation for fraudulent accounts even after it has been established that you are the victim of identity theft.

Criminal Misidentification

Usually, when you hear a professional athlete discussing his contract say, "It's not about the money," there is one thing of which you can be sure: It's about the money. But when it comes to identity theft, it often is not about the money. The problems encountered by someone whose identity has been stolen by a criminal, who then commits crimes in the name of the identity theft victim, are substantial. They involve much more than money.

Hoisted with His Own Petard

James Perry, being concerned that his four drunk driving convictions in Florida would interfere with his application for a Connecticut driver's license, stole the identity of his neighbor, Robert Kowalski. Perry managed to get a Connecticut driver's license and credit cards in the name of Robert Kowalski. Everything was going fine for Perry until he was arrested on a minor disorderly conduct charge. In accordance with standard operating procedure, Kowalski's name was put through a background check for outstanding warrants, and the search indicated that Robert Kowalski was a convicted sex offender who had failed to register in Connecticut as required by state law. Suddenly, Perry decided that it was better to be James Perry than Robert Kowalski and he confessed to his crime. An FBI fingerprint check confirmed his true identity, and he was promptly charged with criminal impersonation.

Arrest Gone to Pot

During a routine traffic stop in Marietta, Ohio, police found that Shaun Saunders had eight pounds of marijuana in his possession. Bail was set at $15,000 and Saunders was promptly released on bail when someone came to court and put up the full bail amount in cash. When Saunders failed to appear for a preliminary hearing, he was indicted by a grand jury. A few months later, police in Bluefield, Virginia, notified Marietta police that they had Saunders in custody. In fact, they were holding Shaun Saunders. The only problem was that FBI fingerprint identification confirmed that the man who had been stopped and arrested by Ohio police was not Shaun Saunders, whose wallet with identifying information had been stolen a year earlier.

It's Not Just the Money

One of the more insidious forms of identity theft occurs when an identity thief not only uses your identity to steal from you or harm your credit, but also commits crimes using your name. Derek Bond, a 72-year-old British retired charity worker, was arrested and held in a South African jail for two weeks awaiting extradition to the United States on an FBI arrest warrant. The FBI did not admit that it had made a mistake in detaining Derek Bond until the real criminal, Derek Sikes, was arrested in Las Vegas. Derek Sikes might have been using Derek Bond's identity for as long as 14 years before the unfortunate Derek Bond became aware of the theft of his good name.

But as bad as Bond's case was, Malcolm Byrd's was even worse. Byrd's troubles began when he read in the local newspaper that he had been arrested on drug charges. He promptly contacted the police, who quickly determined that Byrd was the victim of identity theft. The newspaper even printed a retraction, clarifying the situation. You would think that that would be the end of the story. But unfortunately for Malcolm Byrd, it was not. Barely four months after he thought he had straightened out the matter, he was arrested on the same drug charges. He was released later that day when it again became apparent to the police that Byrd was the victim, not the perpetrator. Over the next five years, his problems continued to mount. First, he was fired when his employer mistakenly accused him of misrepresenting his criminal record. Then he was denied unemployment benefits because of his criminal record that, in truth, never existed. His driver's license was suspended for unpaid traffic tickets he never received. One by one, Malcolm Byrd managed to correct all these mistakes, but his own name continues to haunt him. Finally, while at home with his children, he was arrested and charged with cocaine possession with intent to distribute. Despite his fervent efforts, the Rock County Wisconsin sheriff's officers remained convinced that he was the man they wanted. They continued to remain convinced for the two days he had to stay in jail until the proof of his true identity was established, at least for the moment, and he was released.

Carlos Gomez

Florida resident Carlos Gomez sued Wells Fargo Bank for malicious prosecution relating to an incident of criminal identity theft. Gomez was falsely arrested in a predawn raid at his home in Kendall, Florida, for crimes never committed by him that were actually done by a bank employee at a local Wachovia Bank (Wachovia is now owned by Wells Fargo) where Gomez had a bank account. The rogue employee stole Gomez's identity to launder more than a million dollars he had stolen from the accounts of other bank customers. It took seven months for the identity theft to be discovered and for Gomez to be cleared of all charges. In his lawsuit, Gomez accused the bank of being lax in its security procedures.

What Should You Do If You Are the Victim of Criminal Identity Theft?

Becoming a victim of criminal identity theft can harm you far more than becoming a victim of identity theft through a stolen credit card. It is therefore critical that you take the following steps to minimize the damage:

- Act as soon as you become aware of the problem. Hire a lawyer and contact the police and the District Attorney's office to straighten out the matter. File a report indicating that you are the victim of identity theft. It will be necessary for you to confirm your own identity through photographs and fingerprints. In addition, show your driver's license or passport, or any other identification that you might have that contains your photograph, to law enforcement authorities.

- Get a letter from the District Attorney explaining the situation to have available if you are ever stopped for a traffic violation and your record is checked. The states of Arkansas, Delaware, Iowa, Maryland, Mississippi, Montana, Nevada, Ohio, Oklahoma, and Virginia have Identity Theft Passport Programs. Through these programs, anyone whose identity has been appropriated by someone who uses it in the commission of a crime can, upon proving his identity, receive an Identity Theft Passport. The Identity Theft Passport protects the person and confirms his true identity if there is a question about his criminal responsibility. Even if your state does not have an Identity Theft Passport program, obtain from the law enforcement agency that arrested the person using your name a "clearance letter" or "certificate of release" which indicates that you have not committed the crimes that were the subject of the arrest of the identity theft who used your name. Keep these documents with you at all times.

- Make sure your criminal record is expunged.

- Consider changing your name.
- Consider changing your Social Security number.

Taxes and Identity Theft

Taxes and identity theft seem like a match made in hell. Taxes are bad enough, but piling on identity theft compounds the misery. Whether it is being victimized by a tax-preparing identity thief or falling prey to an identity theft scam that uses phony forms to lure you into providing your Social Security number and other sensitive information, the result is the same: trouble.

The good news, according to the IRS, is that their crack teams of forensic accountants prevented the payments of $1.5 billion in fraudulent tax refund checks last year. The bad news is that the Treasury Inspector General for Tax Administration predicts that the IRS will pay more than $21 billion in fraudulent tax refund checks over the next five years.

The Treasury Inspector General's report also found that the IRS's best efforts in stopping income tax identity theft did not manage to stop it from issuing more than a million dollars in refund checks for 741 separate income tax returns that all used the same Belle Glade, Florida, address, nor did it prevent the IRS from sending checks totaling more than $3.3 million related to 2,137 returns that all listed the same Lansing, Michigan, address. In fact, the report found that the top five addresses used for filing fraudulent returns were sent a total of 4,864 tax refunds totaling more than $8 million related to those fraudulent returns.

Indeed, Florida, the state that leads the country in total identity theft, also has the two top cities from which fraudulent income tax returns were filed, namely, Tampa and Miami.

In addition, in Congressional testimony in 2013, Treasury Inspector General for Tax Administration J. Russell George noted that the IRS still was not in compliance with direct-deposit regulations requiring tax refunds to be deposited into bank accounts only when the name on the bank account matched the name of the tax-filer. In one instance, $909,267 in refunds were sent to a single bank account related to 590 separate income tax returns.

In its investigation, the General Accountability Office found that in 2013 alone there were 915,000 cases of income tax identity theft with an additional 480,000 cases involving fraudulent refund claims using the Social Security numbers of Puerto Rican citizens who generally are not required to file federal income tax returns.

IRS Commissioner John Koskinen has said, "We're now sending a strong message that if you get caught—and we're chasing you hard—and you get convicted, the sentence is not just a month or two. People are going away for 10 to

20 years." All of that might be true and the IRS certainly has increased its efforts to stop income tax identity theft, but with more than 290,000 complaints of income tax identity theft in 2013, a year in which the IRS managed to get only 800 convictions, it would appear that only 0.2 percent of the income tax identity thieves heard Commissioner's Koskinen's strong message.

Particularly prized by identity thieves are the Social Security numbers of children and the elderly who might not have sufficient taxable income required to file a federal income tax return. These numbers therefore are particularly valuable to identity thieves because there won't be a legitimate income tax return filed to alert the IRS to the problem. It is for the same reason that Social Security numbers for citizens of Puerto Rico are also of great value to identity thieves, because citizens of Puerto Rico are required to have Social Security numbers but are not required to file a federal income tax return if their income is derived from Puerto Rico. Even dead people are common victims of identity theft as their names and Social Security numbers continue to be readily available to anyone through the federal government's Death Master File, although legislation was passed in December of 2013 to stop making this information available to the public.

Don't feel bad if you become a victim of identity theft. It can happen to anyone. In 2014, Yafait Tadesse and Eyaso Adebe, two men from Georgia, were convicted of charges of income tax identity theft involving filing a false income tax return using the name of United States Attorney General Eric Holder.

According to Senator Bill Nelson of Florida, "Instead of stealing cars or selling illegal drugs, more and more criminals are looking with envy at the ease with which tax fraud can be committed anonymously. All the fraudster has to do is file a false return electronically and then have the tax refund loaded onto a prepaid debit card."

IRS Vulnerability

Meanwhile, the IRS itself is a ripe target for identity thieves. According to a Government Accountability Office study in 2011, the IRS uses unencrypted protocols for tax processing and is extremely vulnerable to identity theft. A study six years earlier by the GAO that also uncovered security weaknesses in the IRS that could readily be exploited by identity thieves made a series of recommendations for remedying the situation and increasing security, but when the GAO revisited the IRS's data security, it found that only 15 percent of the recommendations of the GAO had been implemented.

The Core of the Problem and an Easy Solution

Identity thieves will use your name and Social Security number to file a fraudulent tax return along with phony income and tax-withholding data in order to collect a refund. If they file a return before you do, upon the filing of your return, you have just guaranteed an audit to process your return manually, carefully checking everything in your return to make sure that your own income tax return is legitimate. At best, this can delay the return to you of any real refund owed you by months at the earliest.

Part of the problem is due to the fact that the IRS tries to process refunds as quickly as possible. Although employers are required to provide W-2 forms and 1099 forms to you no later than the end of January, they are not required to file this information with the federal government until the end of March. Even then, employers are not required to file these forms with the IRS, but instead are required to file them with the Social Security Administration, which does not get around to forwarding them to the IRS until late July. Therefore, the IRS does not cross-reference the real W-2s with those filed by identity thieves until months after the IRS has already sent out a refund to the identity thief. All that the IRS would have to do in order to dramatically reduce income tax identity theft is follow the recommendations of the General Accountability Office and require employers to file their W-2s with the IRS at the same time that they file them with the Social Security Administration and match them up before sending out a refund.

Identity thieves have the refunds sent to post office boxes or have the funds electronically transferred to Green Dot or Walmart money cards that are the equivalent of cash.

Identity thieves are more apt to file their returns electronically because then they don't even have to include a phony W-2.

TIP

File your return early even if you owe money, and then send in your check later, by the April 15th filing deadline.

Protecting Yourself from Income Tax Identity Theft with Form 8821

File an IRS Form 8821 with the IRS. This form is like a power of attorney in that it authorizes the IRS to send to a third party, such as your accountant or lawyer, any information regarding your income tax return. Traditionally, this form has been used when someone is being audited or is having health issues such that an accountant or a lawyer is acting on behalf of the taxpayer with the IRS. However, you can use this form to help combat identity theft. Name yourself as the third party to receive information about your income tax return so that if there are any issues with the phony income tax return filed by the identity thief, you will be contacted. This can help serve as an early-alert system if an identity thief has filed an income tax return on your behalf and the tax return has any issues that arouse IRS interest.

Black Market for Social Security Numbers

There exists an extensive black market for Social Security numbers, with illegal immigrants often purchasing these stolen Social Security numbers to make it easier to get a job. Regina Huerta of Omaha, Nebraska, learned this the hard way. After her purse was stolen, she didn't think much of it. She got a new ATM card and a duplicate Social Security card, but she never reported the theft to the police. It wasn't until years later that she was told by the IRS that a W-2 form filed by a company in California showed that she had earned income in California. At first, she thought it was just a bureaucratic mistake, but when she later learned that records also showed her working in Wisconsin, Utah, Iowa, Missouri, and Arkansas all at the same time, she realized what had happened. Apparently she caught on more quickly than the IRS, which continued to hound her for income tax payments on money she had never earned or received, for ten years.

IRS Efforts

Since 2008, the IRS has put a greater effort into assisting victims of identity theft, including the creation of a special victims unit to help the victims of identity theft; however, the IRS's efforts have been slow. A report of the Treasury Inspector General for Tax Administration Office of Audit in May of 2012 concluded that "the IRS is not effectively providing assistance to victims of identity theft and current processes are not adequate to communicate identity theft procedures to taxpayers resulting in increased burden for victims of identity theft." The report made eight specific recommendations that the IRS has agreed to implement, but only time will tell.

Tax Preparation and Identity Theft

Preparing your income tax return can be taxing enough. Becoming a victim of identity theft in the process seems like cruel and unusual punishment. Many people go to commercial tax preparers who often set up in large rooms in malls or sections of larger stores. At times, the privacy and security of your information is not as protected as it should be. Identity thieves lurking in these places can see documents and information on computer screens. The solution is to always be conscious of maintaining the privacy of your documents and information. Of course, this applies when you are discarding any documents that you might have used to prepare your tax returns. Your trash might be treasure to an identity thief. Thoroughly shred any financial worksheets or documents used to help prepare your income taxes when discarding them.

Just as you should be wary of a free lunch, you should be wary of free tax-filing services as well. Many tax scams originate with the scammers offering free tax-filing services. One of these services, which claimed to be approved by the IRS but in actuality was an unapproved group of scammers in the country of Belarus, adjusted the returns to provide for fraudulently large refunds, with the funds being sent to the scammers rather than the innocent taxpayers.

IRS Scam

In this scam, the identity thief sends you a phony e-mail that says it is from the IRS asking for personal information as a part of an audit. By now, you should know the drill. Do not give it out. The IRS does not use e-mail to contact taxpayers.

IRS Refund Scam

Another common IRS scam involves an e-mail that you receive purportedly from the IRS informing you, "After the last annual calculation of your fiscal activity we have determined that you are eligible to receive a tax return of $253.04. To receive your return, you need to register for an e-Services account: Click here to register. If you already have an e-Services account click here to login." If you are knowledgeable, you will know that a tax refund is not referred to as a "return" by the IRS. If you fall for the bait, you will not get any money from the IRS, but clicking on either link will result in your unwittingly downloading dangerous keystroke-logging malware onto your computer that will enable the identity thief to steal all the information from your computer such as your credit card numbers, Social Security number, passwords, and financial account information, ultimately resulting in your becoming a victim of identity theft.

If you receive an e-mail from the IRS, you can immediately ignore and delete it because the IRS does not initially communicate with taxpayers through e-mail. They use only regular mail to communicate with taxpayers. It is also important to remember that you never should click on links in e-mails, tweets, or text messages because even if the source appears legitimate, you cannot be sure that it is indeed legitimate. It is also possible that the legitimate source of the e-mail, tweet, or text message might have had their account hacked into so that you would trust the communication and click on the link. If you have any concerns about the legitimacy of a forwarded link, contact the person or entity sending it to you by phone to confirm its accuracy. Finally, as a last line of protection, you should make sure not only that you have a good firewall and computer security software, but that it is constantly updated in order to protect you from the latest viruses and other malware.

IRS E-Services Scam

The IRS has warned people about a scam that uses a website that appears to be the e-Services online registration page of the IRS. The real IRS e-Services website does not provide anything for individual taxpayers but does provide Web-based products and information for professional tax preparers. Many people are fooled by phony IRS websites that have URLs that are close to the IRS's URL of www.irs.gov. Some might have "IRS" in the URL, but end in ".com," ".net," or ".org." The only official IRS website is www.irs.gov. This scam is a phishing scam in which the identity thief tricks people into providing their Social Security number or other information.

Remember, if it were the IRS contacting you, they would already have your Social Security number, and they don't need or ask for your bank account information.

Refund Deposit Scams

Another scam starts with a phony e-mail sent to you that purports to be from the IRS informing you that there has been a problem with your tax return and that you need to provide banking information in order to have your refund deposited electronically into your bank account. The e-mail looks official and carries an exact copy of the IRS logo, but it is a phony. If you look closely at the e-mail address from which it was sent, you will notice it reads "administration@ ris.com." The name IRS does not even appear in the e-mail address. If you fall for this scam and make the mistake of providing your bank account information, you will find that money will not be deposited into your account. Rather, your bank account will be emptied by the identity thief who posed as the IRS. Remember, the IRS will not contact you by e-mail. If you are contacted by an e-mail purporting to be from the IRS, it is a scam.

IRS Collection Scam

In 2014, the IRS warned taxpayers of a particularly invasive tax scam that cost unwary taxpayers millions of dollars. The scam involved telephone calls purporting to be from IRS collectors who threatened the victims that they could be arrested, be deported, lose their business, or lose their driver's license if they did not immediately pay an overdue tax bill by credit card or prepaid card such as a Green Dot card. Victims of this scam who had Caller ID found that these calls appeared to be coming from the IRS because the scammers, using a technique called "spoofing," managed to fool the victim's Caller ID. The key to avoiding this scam is merely to be aware that the IRS will not initiate contact with you for anything by telephone or e-mail. If you receive such a call or e-mail, you can disregard it immediately.

Dangers in Tax Software

Tax preparation software such as TurboTax or H&R Block can make filing your income tax return much easier, but it can potentially make you an easy target for identity theft if you are not careful.

With more than 24 million people using just TurboTax, identity thieves can send out phony e-mails purporting to be from TurboTax that can trick you into providing your personal information. This problem is magnified by the fact that unlike the IRS, which will never contact you by e-mail, TurboTax will in fact communicate with you through e-mail. However, the key thing to remember is that neither TurboTax nor H&R Block will ever ask you for personal information through an e-mail, nor will they ask you to update or confirm personal information.

Tips for Using Tax Software

Many people find that it is both easy and convenient to use tax software to prepare their own income tax returns. However, to protect yourself from identity theft, you should follow these steps when using tax software:

- Never open an attachment to an e-mail unless you have confirmed that it is legitimate.
- Never provide personal information in response to an e-mail purportedly from a tax software company.
- Never download software updates that are provided in e-mails. If there are updates, you should download those only from the tax software company's website, which you should access independently and not from a link in an e-mail.

Puerto Rican Tax Scam

Citizens of Puerto Rico are not required to pay federal income taxes, and therefore tax returns filed with the Social Security numbers of Puerto Ricans are less likely to be scrutinized carefully by the IRS. To the IRS, a new tax return from a Puerto Rican citizen can merely appear as if that person had just moved to the mainland U.S. and started earning income there. For more than five years identity thieves stole the Social Security numbers of Puerto Rican citizens and used them to file phony federal income tax returns. In some instances, they joined rogue mail carriers in the scheme to intercept refund checks derived from the phony returns. Between October 2010 and June 2011, the IRS identified phony tax returns using the Social Security numbers of Puerto Rican citizens that would have resulted in $5.6 billion of phony refunds. How much the IRS actually sent out in refunds for the phony tax returns they did not catch is unknown, but has been estimated as being about $2 billion. Generally, the refunds were in the range of $5,000 to $7,000. Stolen Puerto Rican Social Security numbers are sold on the black market for between $8 and $10.

In September of 2011, a former mail carrier, Carmelo Rosado, Jr., was convicted of being a part of one of these schemes.

Trouble in Tampa

Common criminals in Tampa, Florida, who might previously have spent their time selling drugs and robbing houses, have moved on in great numbers into income tax fraud and identity theft—and with good reason. It is simpler, less risky, and more lucrative. Law enforcement officials in Florida estimated that criminals were using stolen Social Security numbers to steal hundreds of millions of dollars. Postal agents managed to retrieve about a hundred million dollars in refund checks sent in response to phony tax returns in Tampa. Tampa Police Chief Jane Castor estimated that amount to be about 10 percent of the total amount resulting from tax fraud and identity theft in her city.

Brazen Tampa criminals even rented out a social club to instruct criminals in how to use identity theft and prepare fraudulent income tax returns. In return, the teachers received a percentage of the "profits." The atmosphere was actually festive as they would throw tax-filing parties.

Holly M. Barnes

Holly M. Barnes was convicted of filing false income tax returns and identity theft after she stole information she had access to as a Girl Scout leader to obtain personal information about the Girl Scouts in her troop. She created a phony form titled "Girl Scout Medical Release," which included Social Security numbers for the Scouts, and harvested that information to file phony income tax returns that brought her more than $187,000 in false income tax refunds. The form she created was not an official Girl Scout form, and there was no need for the girls to have to provide their Social Security numbers.

Cora Cadia Ford

Cora Cadia Ford was convicted of income tax identity theft. Among the people whose identities she stole were people who were homeless and people with disabilities. As a result of her crimes, many of the victims had their Social Security Disability Income payments reduced or eliminated until the scam was resolved. One victim's SSDI benefits were reduced to approximately $27 per month as a result of Ford's crimes, leaving the victim without enough money to pay for her medications.

Tax Fraud by Prisoners

According to a Treasury Department report issued in 2012, the number of prisoners filing false tax returns has doubled in the past five years. In addition, the amount of phony refunds paid to prisoners filing these returns has more than tripled to $39.1 billion. According to the study, almost 45,000 phony income tax returns were filed by prisoners in 2009. Prisoners in Florida, Georgia, and California lead the country in the number of filings of false income tax returns. Unfortunately, we cannot estimate the true amount stolen by prisoners from the federal government through false income tax returns because, according to the Treasury Department report, the IRS does not properly audit all the income tax returns filed by prisoners.

The most common ways that prisoners file phony tax returns is by getting the names and Social Security numbers of other people, including fellow prisoners, and then filing tax returns seeking large refunds. In some instances the prisoners would research online for businesses that have gone bankrupt, which assists in making it more difficult for the IRS to verify the accuracy of the reported income.

Daniel Suarez, a Florida prisoner, was convicted of filing 14 false income tax returns and getting more than $58,000 in refunds. Upon his conviction, five years were added to his sentence.

More Identity Theft Tax Scams to Avoid

People have been receiving a form and cover letter by way of a fax purportedly from the IRS in which the victim is told that updated information is needed by the IRS in order to deposit a tax refund to the recipient's bank account. The form is called a "Certificate of Current Status of Beneficial Owner for United States Tax Recertification and Withholding." The form asks for detailed personal information, including bank account information and PIN numbers, that can be used to steal your identity and the money out of your accounts. There is no such form and the IRS never asks for such information.

Another scam involves an e-mail purportedly from the Taxpayer Advocate Service, which actually is a part of the IRS. The real Taxpayer Advocate Service helps taxpayers resolve disputes with the IRS. The phony Taxpayer Advocate Service e-mail, however, asks for personal information including mother's maiden name, PIN number, bank account numbers, and more. By completing and submitting the form, the victim is told that he or she will receive a tax refund. The truth is that if you provide the requested information, you will become a victim of identity theft. Refunds are claimed only through your annual tax return. No other form is used and the IRS will, again, never ask for such personal information.

Bad spelling and grammar are always a warning signal of a scam. Another tax scam that is prevalent starts with an e-mail you receive from the "IRS Antifraud Comission." Apparently identity thieves have trouble spelling the word "Commission." The taxpayer is told that someone has enrolled the taxpayer's credit card with the IRS for payment of income taxes. To make things worse, the taxpayer is told that there have also been security breaches with the taxpayer's bank account and that "remaining founds" instead of "funds" are frozen. In order to correct these problems, the taxpayer is instructed to click on a link that asks for personal information, which is used to make the taxpayer a victim of both identity theft and bad spelling.

Tax-Filing Tips

Income tax identity theft is a huge problem, but by taking the following precautions, you can dramatically reduce your chances of becoming a victim of income tax identity theft:

- Protect your W-2 and other forms with personal information that you need in order to prepare your income tax return, but that can result in your becoming a victim of tax identity theft if they fall into the hands of an identity thief.

- If you decide to have your income tax return prepared by a professional tax preparer, make sure that you have checked out the tax preparer well to make sure that they are legitimate. In addition, even if you choose an honest tax preparer, their computers can be hacked and make you a victim of tax identity theft, too. So ask them what steps they take to protect the security of your information in their computers and in their files.

- If you are e-filing on your own, make sure that you use a strong password. After you have filed, it is a good idea to put the tax return on a CD or flash drive that you keep in a secure place and then remove the information from your computer's hard drive. This will protect you if your computer is hacked.

- If you are e-filing on your own, make sure that your firewall and security software is current.

- If you use regular mail to file your income tax return, mail it directly from the post office rather than leaving it in a mailbox from where it could be stolen.

- If you are getting a refund, you should consider having your refund sent electronically to your bank account rather than having a check that can be stolen sent to you through the mail.

- File early. Identity thieves file early in order to steal your refund before you have a chance to file.

Steps to Take If You Are a Victim of Tax Identity Theft

Despite their best efforts, many people become victims of income tax identity theft. If this happens to you, you should take the following steps:

- File a report with the Federal Trade Commission's identity theft database.
- Call the Federal Trade Commission's hotline for personal identity theft counseling at 877-ID-THEFT (438-4338).
- Put a credit freeze on your credit report with each of the three major credit-reporting agencies.
- Call the Identity Protection Specialized Unit of the IRS at 800-908-4490.
- File with the IRS an IRS Identity Theft Affidavit Form 14039.

Identity Theft and Investments

Frank Gruttadauria was a successful investment broker who handled millions of dollars on behalf of his wealthy clients. He was also an identity thief who was convicted of securities fraud, wire fraud, bank fraud, and identity theft that made his clients much less wealthy. His easy access to not only his clients' personal information but also their actual accounts made his crimes both easier to accomplish and more frightening to people who already feel quite vulnerable. The Ohio-based Gruttadauria stole $125 million from his clients' accounts, shifting money from one client's account to another and all the time keeping plenty for himself.

TIP

Read your monthly brokerage account statements carefully. Look for anything out of the ordinary. Make sure your broker explains anything to you that you do not understand. Get a second opinion. A certified financial planner might be able to better review your statement for you and perhaps, as an added bonus, even make suggestions that might include tax advice pertaining to your investments with expertise that your broker might not necessarily possess.

Also, ask the branch manager of the investment company with which you do business about its policies for reviewing and overseeing the actions of their individual brokers. This should be done on a regular basis.

Jury Duty

Comedian Norm Crosby said that he did not like the idea of trusting his fate to 12 people who were not smart enough to get out of jury duty. Jury duty is a civic duty, like voting, that we should embrace. At least, that is the theory. Unfortunately, it would be naïve to fail to recognize that many people consider jury duty an annoyance and a disturbance of their everyday lives to be avoided whenever possible. Identity thieves know this. One identity theft scam involves the thief posing as a court worker placing telephone calls to people. During those phone calls, he tells his victims that the records indicate that the person being called has failed to report for jury duty. The identity thief then asks the potential victims to provide their Social Security numbers and other personal information. And then, as they say, the game begins.

Battling the Companies with Which You Do Business

It is certainly disheartening to be a victim of identity theft, but having to battle with the companies with which you regularly do business following the discovery of your identity being compromised is almost beyond comprehension.

"The Same Old Watson! You Never Learn That the Gravest Issues Might Depend upon the Smallest Things."

This quote comes from Sherlock Holmes in *The Adventures of the Creeping Man*. It also could describe the unfortunate misadventures of another John Watson of more recent ilk. John Watson first learned that he had been a victim of identity theft when he noticed that $7,600 had been taken from his Bank of America bank account. After a Holmesian investigation, he learned that an identity thief had opened a PayPal account in Watson's name and was able to get at money from Watson's bank account to pay for purchases using PayPal. You would think that after this became apparent, Watson would be in the clear. However, John Watson was in for an expensive lesson. Although the money had been taken from his account six months earlier, Watson did not first learn of the money being missing from his Bank of America account for six months because he had been traveling extensively out of town. Watson's problem was compounded by the fact that, compared with credit card laws pertaining to responsibility for unauthorized use, the laws governing electronic transfers do not provide as much protection. As I indicated earlier, with an electronic transfer, if you notify the institution within 2 days that your account has been accessed improperly, your liability is limited to $50. If your report of the theft is made between 3 and 60 days after the theft, your responsibility for unauthorized charges is limited to $500. But if your report of unauthorized use is made more than 60 days after the theft occurs, the law sets no limit to your financial responsibility. Yikes! This problem can be particularly troublesome with identity theft because most victims of identity theft do not learn that they are victims until long after the theft has occurred.

PayPal and Watson's other pal, Bank of America, were not terribly cooperative with John Watson over this matter, or perhaps that is exactly what they were— terribly cooperative. With some effort, Watson was able to convince PayPal to return to him the $2,100 that remained in the fraudulent PayPal account that had been set up in Watson's name by the identity thief who had victimized him. But this still left John Watson $5,500 in the hole. When negotiating and pleading with both Bank of America and PayPal went nowhere, Watson took his case to the bargain basement of the law: small claims court. He sued both Bank of America and PayPal for his remaining loss of $5,500. Acting as his own attorney, he argued that despite the laws regarding electronic transactions, PayPal was negligent in not notifying him more promptly that a fraud had occurred. A sympathetic judge ruled in John Watson's favor. The tale has a bittersweet ending. Because the limit on a small claims court action was $5,000, the checks John Watson received from Bank of America and PayPal were limited to $2,500 from each. He ended up forfeiting $500. Still, all in all, John Watson handled himself in a way that would have made Sherlock Holmes proud.

6

Protecting Your Privacy—A Key to Preventing Identity Theft

A key to preventing identity theft is limiting the exposure of as much data about you as possible. Identity thieves exploit the availability of personal information from free websites throughout the Internet, as well as by hacking into the companies and agencies that hold personal information about us. Unfortunately, not enough of us consider this even though we know that the more places that have information about us, the greater the possibility of identity theft occurring through hacking and other actions over which we have no control. According to Consumer Reports, almost half of the victims of identity theft became victims not because of their own actions, but because their personal information had been stolen or hacked from companies, government agencies, and others who store our personal information. Regardless of how vigilant you are about protecting your privacy, your information is only as safe as the many places that store that information. As my grandmother used to say, "I can keep a secret; it is the people I tell who can't keep a secret."

Protecting Your Privacy on Facebook

Consumer Reports has estimated that of 900 million users of Facebook, only about 13 million use or are even aware of Facebook's privacy controls. In 2011, the Federal Trade Commission required Facebook to be more transparent about its privacy policy because, according to the FTC, Facebook "deceived customers by telling them they could keep their information on Facebook private and then repeatedly allowing it to be shared and made public." In response, Facebook CEO Mark Zuckerberg pledged to do better and committed to making "Facebook the leader in transparency and control around privacy."

Facebook Quizzes

Social networking is as the name implies—social. One of the common uses of Facebook is for quizzes. Unfortunately, one of the side effects of quizzes is the gathering of information on you as a taker of the quiz. At the start of a quiz, a notice will come up informing you that in order to take the quiz, you assent to providing access to information about you. However, the notice also will inform you that you have the right to change your mind and opt out or cancel taking the quiz in order to protect the privacy of your information. The information you provide if you take the quiz will include not only your profile information, but photographs and even information on your friends. The American Civil Liberties Union (ACLU) has been quite critical of this practice.

Privacy Settings on Facebook

Facebook, by its very nature, is a place for sharing information; however, as the figures provided by Consumer Reports indicate, few people are aware of or exercise their rights to limit their information on Facebook by consciously utilizing its privacy settings. This is further complicated by the fact that Facebook has frequently changed its privacy settings. For each of the settings on your Facebook account, you can set your privacy settings to share the information with selected groups of people. At the bottom of every Facebook page is a link to Facebook's privacy page where you can find information about Facebook's latest privacy functions. You might want to classify more people as "acquaintances" who will have more limited access to personal information you post. You should deliberately determine what information you want to share and with whom. Personal information such as your birth date, your place of employment, and the names of relatives can be used by identity thieves to help make you a victim of identity theft. Sharing information too extensively could expose your data to large numbers of people whom you might not want to have your information.

To limit access to some of your profile information, such as your birth date, relationship status, or employer, all you need to do is click on the Update Info button in the box below the Timeline cover photograph, which will take you to where you can restrict access as you like.

It is important to remember that your Facebook name and profile photograph will always be available to anyone. For greater privacy, some people choose a profile photograph that is not of their face. You also can use a name different from your real name as your Facebook name for increased privacy.

If you are among the people who have never used the privacy settings, most likely all of your status updates have been set to Public by default. You might want to go through your posted personal information and limit the audience for the items you would prefer to restrict.

Unwittingly, your friends might share information about you with identity thieves. Without your knowledge or your friend's knowledge, an app that a friend uses could get access to your information. Fortunately, however, you can prevent this by turning off all apps, which will prevent all apps your friends use from being able to gain access to your information. However, this draconian action will also prevent you from being able to use any games, apps, or other sites available on Facebook. To create an app for Facebook, all you need is a Facebook account, a cellphone number, and a credit card. Identity thieves can certainly supply all of that.

You might want to regularly check your Facebook page to see how it appears to others and perhaps adjust your privacy settings. It is a good idea to go to the Facebook privacy guide on a regular basis to make sure that you are not sharing more information than you want and to also make sure you are up to date with the latest Facebook privacy feature updates. Here is a link to the Facebook privacy guide: https://www.facebook.com/help/445588775451827.

It is important to remember that it is up to you to take action to protect your privacy on Facebook. Because of Facebook's business model, the more information it provides its advertisers, the more advertising dollars it pulls in. Facebook's interests in profits do not necessarily coincide with what might be your desire for privacy.

Protecting Your Privacy on Google

Most websites and search engines, such as Google, Yahoo!, and Bing, use cookies. Cookies track your Internet usage and the websites you go to. They are used by search engines to tailor advertising to your interests; however, they also can be used by identity thieves to produce more enticing phishing websites. If you do not want to receive cookies when you go to Google, you can change your browser's setting to refuse cookies in general or from specific websites.

Dangers of Data Gatherers

With so much personal information available on the Internet, companies have arisen that gather this information, and for fees of between $2 and $50 these companies provide anyone who asks and is willing to pay for it with your name, address, age, telephone number, home's value if you own one, previous addresses, previous criminal convictions, educational background, occupation, hobbies, and more. These data-gathering companies primarily provide this information to advertisers, because the more they know about you, the more they can efficiently target specific advertising to your own preferences. But this information can also be misused by identity thieves, making it easier for them to trick you into providing the remaining information they need in order to make you a victim of identity theft.

For those who are particularly security-conscious, there are four software programs that will provide you with greater security while you use the Internet, and prevent data collectors from following you online. Abine (www.abine.com) has a free version and other versions for additional fees that will let you block cookies. It works with Mozilla Firefox, Internet Explorer, Google Chrome, and Safari browsers. AdBlock Plus (www.adblockplus.org) is free and blocks out all advertising. It is available for the Mozilla Firefox, Google Chrome, Opera, Android, and Internet Explorer browsers. Better Privacy (www.betterprivacy. en.softonic.com) is free and prevents hidden flash cookies from storing information about you, but it works only with Mozilla Firefox. Finally, Disconnect (www.disconnect.me) blocks both ads and social network tracking. It also permits you to use Google without being tracked.

Do Not Track

Many people are pushing for a federal law that would require websites and browsers to tell you when you are being tracked and to provide a Do Not Track list for which you could enroll, similar to the Do Not Call List to stop telemarketers from calling you. Passage of such a law in the short run is not likely.

However, unbeknown to many people who use later versions of Internet Explorer, Safari, Opera, Chrome, and Mozilla Firefox as Internet browsers, these browsers already provide Do Not Track capabilities, which take no more effort than just choosing the capability as an option on your toolbar.

Actions to Take to Increase Your Privacy

There are several affirmative actions we can take to increase our privacy and make us less susceptible to identity theft. Here are some of the most important ones:

- The credit-reporting agencies regularly sell names and addresses to other businesses that will solicit your business. You can prevent your name and address from being sold by the credit-reporting agencies to other businesses by calling 888-5OPTOUT (567-8688). Among other things, this will have you taken off of the lists for the so-called "preapproved" credit cards, which pose a particular danger of identity theft if the mailing is intercepted by an identity thief.
- To be taken off of the Direct Marketing Association's own list, which is the source of much of your junk mail, go to https://www.dmachoice. org/register.php, where you can first register your name and address and then have it placed on a "do not mail" list. There is no cost to register or to be placed on the "do not mail" list.

- If, like many of us, you have ever purchased something through a catalog, your information has been shared with other catalog companies through a company called Abacus. You can, however, opt out of the Abacus database and prevent more catalogs from being sent to you by sending an e-mail to abacusoptout@epsilon.com in which you provide your name including your middle initial, your current address, and a request to be removed from their database.

- Don't fill in product registration cards that you get when you purchase consumer goods. The implication is that you need to complete the cards and return them in order to be covered by warranties for the particular goods you have purchased, but that is not the truth. You do not need to register to be covered by a product's warranty. Failing to return the card does not negate your warranty. Your receipt is good enough evidence of the purchase of the particular goods should you need to exercise your warranty rights. However, for products such as car seats, cribs, or other products that might potentially be subject to a safety recall, you might want to return the card so that you can be notified in the event of a recall. In this instance, you should provide only your name, your address, the date of purchase, and the product serial number.

- Carefully evaluate your privacy settings on your social network sites and set them up at a level with which you are comfortable.

- Use the Do Not Track option for your Internet browsing.

7

Security Software

A gigabyte of security software is worth a pound of cure. With so much identity theft tied to identity thieves stealing information through phishing, malware, or otherwise from your computer and other mobile devices, it is important not only that you protect all of these devices, but that you constantly update your security software to make sure that it will protect you from the newest threats. Despite the fact that we do so much on our smartphones, laptops, and other mobile devices, many people who are security-conscious when it comes to protecting their home computer are less apt to consider security software for their laptop or their smartphone.

For computers and laptops, most people will be sufficiently served by any of a number of free security software packages, including these favorites of Consumer Reports:

- Avira, which you can get at www.free-av.com
- AVG, which you can get at www.free.avg.com
- Avast, which you can get at www.avast.com
- Microsoft Security Essentials, which you can get at http://windows. microsoft.com/en-us/windows/security-essentials-download

All of these services provide protection from viruses, spyware, and malware. As always, it is important to make sure you keep your security software up-to-date. It is important to remember, however, that the free software is not as comprehensive as security software for which you pay. The major hacking of Target occurred because a third-party vendor with which it did business used a free version of a popular anti-malware program that was not up to the task of stopping the malware that ultimately resulted in the massive Target data breach.

In addition, it is important to update all your software with the latest security patches as they are issued by the software developers. Identity thieves are constantly discovering and exploiting vulnerabilities in the software programs that we all use, so it is critical to update your software as soon as new updates are provided. The best way to do this is to have updates installed automatically, but you can also sign up to receive regular security updates from the United States Computer Emergency Readiness Team, which is a part of the Department of Homeland Security, by going to www.us-cert.gov.

On April 8, 2014, Microsoft stopped providing security updates and patches for the popular Windows XP operating system. This was not a business tactic designed to get people to purchase newer operating systems, but rather a recognition that, just as your car has a limited life span after which it costs more to fix than to get a newer car, so do computer operating systems have limited life spans, after which it becomes more prudent to replace them rather than continually try to update them. Many individuals, companies, and governmental agencies failed to update their operating systems to the newer Windows 7 and Windows 8 operating systems prior to April 8, 2014, thereby putting them in serious jeopardy as identity thieves exploit newly uncovered security flaws. If you are using Windows XP, it is critical for you to update to a more secure and updated operating system as soon as possible. It is also worth noting that Microsoft has already indicated that it will stop providing security updates for the Windows 7 operating system on January 14, 2020.

Among the pay security software packages, Consumer Reports favored the following:

- Avira, which you can get at http://www.avira.com/en/personal
- G-Data, which you can get at www.gdata-software.com
- Kaspersky which you can get at www.kaspersky.com
- ESET, which you can get at www.eset.com

These services provide additional protection against malware and spam, and include a firewall. Most routers have firewalls already built in, and a firewall is built into your Windows or Mac OS X software as well; however, the firewalls in the pay security software packages might provide some additional protection.

For your smartphone or other mobile devices, you should also have security software specifically installed on these devices. Among the more popular and easy-to-use software packages are these:

- BullGuard Mobile Security, which you can get as either a free version or an enhanced for-pay version at www.bullguard.com
- Kaspersky Mobile Security, which comes in a pay version that you can get at http://usa.kaspersky.com/products-services/home-computer-security/mobile-security
- ESET Mobile Security, which comes in a pay version that you can get at http://www.eset.com/us/home/products/mobile-security/

Again, it is important to keep your smartphone and mobile device security software up-to-date. Finally, beware of advertisements for software that might actually contain the malware that you are trying to protect yourself from. Always confirm online that the software you are using is from a legitimate company and not an identity thief. Go online and check out recommendations. If you have questions about the company's legitimacy, you can also go to Google and put in the name of the company along with the word "scam" and see what comes up.

8

The Dangers of Data Breaches

I dentity theft depends on the security of your personal information. When you provide this information to an identity thief as a result of a phishing scam, you set yourself up for a disastrous identity theft experience. Unfortunately, just as a chain is only as strong as its weakest link, so is the security of your personal information, and in turn your identity, only as safe as the security of the many places that have and store your personal information. Identity thieves are well aware of this and often find it more simple and effective to hack into companies and institutions that store large amounts of personal information on a great many people. Being aware of this threat should make you more hesitant to share your personal information unless absolutely necessary and should make you more vigilant in inquiring as to the security steps taken by these companies and institutions to keep your data secure.

Data breaches can occur through sophisticated computer hacking or pure carelessness, as when unencrypted information is lost when laptops containing such information are lost. Rogue employees with access to either computer or paper records can also be a source of data breaches. In recent years, organized crime, most notably in Eastern Europe, has turned to data breaches as a source of income. A joint study by Verizon and international law enforcement agencies including the U.S. Secret Service showed that organized crime is increasingly becoming involved in data breaches. It is no longer the disgruntled employee or the computer hacker next door. But regardless of who is committing the data breach, the result is the same: an extreme risk of identity theft. Some studies have suggested that as much as 27 percent of all identity theft could be traced back to data breaches.

According to a study by the research firm Risk Based Security in 2013, there were more than 2,000 data breaches affecting an astounding 814 million data records. Disturbingly, according to the Identity Theft Resource Center, the healthcare industry was the sector that had the most data breaches for the first time since such figures began being tracked in 2005.

An indication of the depth of the problem of data breaches is that according to American cybersecurity firm Mandiant, 96 percent of data breaches are not discovered by the victimized companies and governmental agencies hacked, but by third parties such as banks noticing patterns of fraudulent credit card use. Mandiant also found that the data breaches went undiscovered for an average of almost 13 months.

The Black Market

Much of the data stolen by identity thieves through data breaches is now sold to other identity thieves on black market websites that are increasing in number and sophistication. Many of the sales of this information are done using the digital currency Bitcoin.

The price at which stolen credit card information is sold varies considerably from as little as $10 per card to as much as $135 for a credit card issued by a foreign bank. Foreign banks do not do as good a job of monitoring the use of cards to discover fraudulent use and data breaches that might be connected to the fraudulent use. In fact, many of the major data breaches in the United States in recent years, such as those that occurred at Target and Neiman Marcus, were discovered first by banks noticing a pattern in credit cards being fraudulently used.

Just how profitable is this new black market of cybercriminals and identity thieves? According to a recent study by the Rand Corporation, it now exceeds, or soon will, the profits of drug dealing throughout the world.

Illegal Profiting from Credit Card Hacking

Whereas it once took the proverbial computer whiz to write the programs used to hack into the databases of retailers, now identity thieves can purchase the hacking software they need on black market websites along with the technical support that the rest of us have gotten used to having provided when we buy legitimate software. A common method for cashing in on the stolen credit and debit cards is to use those cards to buy gift cards, often from online stores such as Amazon. The gift cards are in turn used to buy products that are easy to resell, such as smartphones or video game consoles. The products are then shipped to an accomplice who, in many instances, has no idea that he or she is participating in a criminal enterprise, but merely had answered an online ad to make money from home by shipping goods under some pretense. The identity thief then sells the merchandise online and notifies his unwitting accomplice where to ship the goods. Under this scenario an identity thief could operate the entire scam entirely from out of the country.

Another way identity thieves profit off of hacking into companies and stealing credit card information is by making counterfeit credit cards and debit cards for the stolen accounts. Counterfeit debit cards are particularly troublesome because they provide direct access to your bank account, and even if you catch the identity theft right away, stolen funds might not be credited back to you for weeks while the bank completes its investigation. Identity thieves will also use the stolen credit cards to purchase gift cards and then sell the gift cards on black market websites to other criminals for around 90 percent of their face value.

Presently, there is no federal law requiring data breach reporting and notification by entities in both the governmental sector and the private sector. California became the first state to require such notifications in 2002. California's lead was followed by 45 other states.

Hacking Is Universal

Late in 2013, Trustwave, a cybersecurity company, uncovered a hacking of close to two million Facebook, Google, Twitter, Yahoo, LinkedIn, and other social media accounts. Even more ominously, the hacking included other Internet sites, such as ADP, a payroll service provider. The hackings appear to have started on October 21, 2013, and were not discovered for a couple of months. Compromised information included usernames and passwords. Hacking is a worldwide phenomenon with computers affected in more than 100 countries. In response to the hacking and data breach ADP, Facebook, LinkedIn, and Twitter notified their users to reset passwords for affected accounts. The hacking was achieved by luring people into downloading keystroke-logging malware that stole the information from their computers. This technique is referred to as phishing, which is described in an earlier chapter in this book.

TIP

Also distressing is the fact that in uncovering this wave of hacking, Trustwave identified the passwords that were compromised and the large majority of them were simple passwords that are easy for identity thieves to guess. The most common of the stolen passwords was 123456. Not only is this a problem because it is an easily guessed password, but also, because too often people use the same password for all of their accounts, an identity thief with access to this password would have the password for other accounts of his or her victim.

LinkedIn

In 2012, the popular business social media company LinkedIn was hacked, resulting in the hacker posting 6.5 million passwords online. In the wake of this major event, identity thieves followed up the hacking with phishing e-mails to LinkedIn's customers that were aimed at obtaining users' login information and passwords. Other phishing schemes attempted to lure users into downloading attachments that contained keystroke-logging malware.

The Lesson

Anytime your password might be compromised due to a hacking, you should immediately change your password. You also should make it a practice to use different passwords for different accounts because if you fail to do so and an identity thief obtains a password that you use universally, all of your various accounts are in jeopardy. Too many people fail to take this important advice. Also, never click on links you receive in an e-mail unless you are positive of its legitimacy. You are generally better off going to the company's website independently, and not through a link, at an address that you know is correct if you need to download anything.

War Driving in Washington

For three years ending in 2011, a small sophisticated group of identity thieves targeted at least 53 businesses in the Puget Sound area of the state of Washington using a drive-by identity theft technology called "war driving" combined with old-style breaking and entering into company offices. In the offices they would secretly install identity theft computer programs on insufficiently protected computers to steal information and up to $3 million.

War driving, which has been used for years by sophisticated identity thieves, involves driving by companies with a Wi-Fi receiver that would pick up the unprotected Wi-Fi signals from inside the walls of these companies used for communication between the companies' computers within the building. The thieves would then hack into the companies' computers and get access to all the information contained in them. Other times, they would physically break into the buildings of targeted companies and steal minor items to cover their true intentions, all the while installing malware on the companies' computers to break their passwords and security codes so that they could access the valuable information contained on these computers.

In some instances, the thieves would take over the payroll systems of the companies, steal the identities of the employees, set up accounts in the names of the employees, and route paychecks to these accounts, which they would then proceed to loot.

In one instance, a company's financial officer became aware that his company had been hacked only when he found an unscheduled payroll printout on his printer that had been generated automatically when the payroll program was used by the hackers. What the financial officer of the hacked company found was two new fictional employees and paychecks that were being routed to bank accounts in North Dakota.

After years of intense police work, the ring was broken. John Earl Griffin, one of the identity thieves, received a sentence of 95 months, and Brad Eugene Lowell received a sentence of 78 months.

Albert Gonzales

Although the war-driving efforts of Griffin and Lowell were impressive, the king of war driving remains Albert Gonzales, who used war driving to steal more than 90 million credit and debit card numbers from TJX, Office Max, Barnes & Noble, and a number of other companies between 2005 and 2008, a time period during which he was a paid undercover informant for the United States Secret Service. After Gonzales obtained the credit card and debit card information, he sent it to computer servers that he leased in Latvia and Ukraine, where Ukrainian Maksym Yastremskiy sold them to identity thieves who took the card data and created counterfeit cards. Yastremskiy was captured in Turkey in 2007, convicted of identity theft, and sentenced by a Turkish Court to 30 years in prison. Following Yastremskiy's arrest, his computer provided American authorities with information that implicated Gonzales. In 2012, Albert Gonzales was sentenced to 20 years in prison, which is the longest sentence in American history for hacking and identity theft.

Credit Card Processors

In recent years as bank security has increased, identity thieves have focused more of their attention on credit card processors, the companies that act as middlemen for retailers, the credit card companies, and the banks dealing with credit card transactions. For as long as two years before being discovered, Heartland Payment Systems had more than 130 million credit and debit card records from 250,000 retailers and restaurants stolen.

Student Loan Information Breach

In 2010, the names, addresses, Social Security numbers, and other personal information of 3.3 million people with student loans was stolen through a data breach at Educational Credit Management Corp, which is a guarantor of federal student loans. The theft of the information was accomplished merely by stealing unencrypted information on a portable media device. A few years earlier 1.7 million records of the Texas Guaranteed Student Loan Corp were stolen in a more sophisticated computer hacking.

Wisconsin Data Breach

In 2012, for the fourth time in six years, the Wisconsin Department of Revenue negligently released personal information on Wisconsin taxpayers, putting them at serious risk of identity theft. In 2012, the Wisconsin DOR put up on its website a report of real estate property sales from 2011, but included for the entire world to see 110,795 Social Security numbers of people involved in those transactions.

Coca-Cola

In 2014, a number of laptops were stolen from the corporate headquarters of Coca-Cola in Atlanta. These laptops had personal data of up to 74,000 people and, most disturbingly, the data had been stored on the laptops totally unencrypted. The laptops were recovered, but the threat of identity theft to the affected people was huge. Among the information on the laptops were the names and Social Security numbers of 18,000 Coca-Cola employees as well as personal information including driver's license numbers on another 54,000 people. This is yet the latest instance of a disturbing trend of companies and government agencies not taking the basic security step of encrypting personal data on portable laptops. NASA has been victimized twice by theft of laptops with sensitive personal information. It shouldn't take a rocket scientist to figure out that this information should be encrypted.

TIP

What can you do to protect yourself from this type of corporate negligence? The first thing you can do is to ask any company that holds personal information about you whether they encrypt the data and, if not, why not. You should also ask about what other security steps they take to preserve the privacy of your information. Finally, you might want to consider putting a credit freeze on your credit report, which will prevent anyone who does get access to your personal data, such as your name and Social Security number, from being able to access your credit report for purposes of utilizing your credit to make a large purchase.

When your personal information is compromised in a data breach, not only are you more susceptible to traditional identity theft, but you can be further victimized by a technique called "spear phishing," which occurs when you get an e-mail that is personally tailored to you from the identity thief posing as another company or even law enforcement with an offer to help you remedy your situation. People are more likely to provide information or even payments for offered assistance when the e-mailed communication from the identity thief looks even more legitimate than usual because it already contains personal information about you, as contrasted with some of the phishing e-mails that we all receive that are generically addressed to "Dear Customer" without any personal information that should be available to the institution purporting to communicate with us. Never trust an e-mail; particularly after you receive one following the hacking of a company with which you do business.

Colleges

As the old saying goes, "Fool me once, shame on you; fool me twice, shame on me." In 2014, the Maricopa County Community College revealed that its computers had been hacked and personal information including Social Security numbers and banking information of more than 2.4 million students, former students, employees, and vendors, covering a period of more than 30 years, was compromised. What makes this security breach even more egregious in this particular case is the fact that Maricopa County Community College was hacked back in 2011, but steps to improve the security of their computer systems were not taken despite the recommendations of employees of the college's information technology department and their warning that the 2011 breach, which affected only 400 people, exposed a flaw that could affect many more people and ultimately did.

Also in 2014, the University of Maryland suffered a data breach that resulted in personal information of more than 300,000 students, faculty, and other university employees connected with the university since 1998 being stolen by computer hackers. In a statement disclosing the data theft, the university said that computer and data security was "a very high priority" of the university, which is hard to believe because of the lax security that led to the data theft. Included in the compromised data were names, Social Security numbers, birth dates, and other information for all faculty, staff, students, and university personnel issued a university identification since 1998. This information is a veritable treasure-trove for hackers who, armed with this information, use it for purposes of identity theft. The University of Maryland is by no means alone when it comes to being hacked. Harvard, Stanford, Cornell, Princeton, Johns Hopkins, the University of Rhode Island, the University of Arizona, Marquette, and more than 50 other colleges and universities have been the victims of data breaches in the past couple of years. The reason for targeting universities and colleges is simple. Generally they maintain tremendous amounts of personal information and their record for data security is not good. Colleges and universities have much personal information that is often easily accessible within the school's computer systems. Too often schools have permitted the information to be on unencrypted laptops and flash drives. In addition, many schools do not have sufficient security programs in place to limit access to personal information, which the universities keep in their computers long after it is necessary to be kept, such as Social Security numbers for students who have long since graduated.

Once again, the situation might not be as bad as it appears—it is far worse. For as Larry Ponemon, chairman of the Ponemon Institute, a privacy and security research group, said, "There are probably a lot of data breaches in higher education that go undetected, probably more so than in other industries."

TIP

Schools have to start giving more than lip service to their commitment to data security. Data-breach-prevention systems should be implemented that include, but are not limited to, updated firewalls, limited access to personal information, purging of unnecessary information, and encryption. Personal information should not be as open and available as it presently is at many universities.

Retailers

Recent years have been difficult ones for retailers, who have been a constant target of hackers looking for personal information to turn into identity theft.

Target

More than 100 million credit and debit cards were stolen in a massive hacking of retailer Target between November 27 and December 15, 2013. The data stolen included customers' names, credit card numbers, debit card numbers, expiration dates, and three-digit security codes found on their cards.

The hacking of Target was accomplished through the initial hacking of Fazio Mechanical, a heating and air conditioning company that does business with Target and had access to Target's computers for billing and ordering purposes. The way that Fazio was hacked was through "spear phishing." In this scam the victim receives an e-mail directed to the person or entity by name that appears legitimate or promises something enticing, such as free videos of a newsworthy or otherwise intriguing event. After the victim clicks on the link in the e-mail or downloads the attachment in the e-mail, malware is downloaded onto the victim's computer that provides access to all the information in that computer, which in this case included the information necessary to access Target's computer system. Even though Fazio's computers were protected by anti-malware programs, either its program was not as good as necessary or it was merely not current with the latest malware threats. Anti-malware software programs are generally at least 30 days behind the latest malware threats.

Sally Beauty Holdings

Sally Beauty Holdings, a multibillion-dollar beauty products retailer with 3,300 stores around the world including 2,600 in the United States, suffered a security breach that compromised the credit cards and debit cards of hundreds of thousands of its customers. Unlike in the case of the data breaches at Target, Neiman Marcus, and Michaels, which occurred around the same time, it appears that Sally Beauty's own cyberdefense technology might have detected the intrusion at the same time that a number of banks identified Sally Beauty Supply as being a victim of a data breach. In the Target, Neiman Marcus, and Michaels data breaches, it was banks that monitored credit cards that first noticed the pattern of stolen cards being tied to the particular retailers. Investigators theorized that the same criminals were behind all of those retail breaches in late 2013 and early 2014, and we should expect more retail breaches in the near future.

FBI Warning

In 2014, the FBI issued a warning to retailers throughout the country informing them that the type of hacking of their credit and debit card payment systems that was used against Target and Neiman Marcus could be expected to be used against many more retailers in the future. The malware used in these attacks infects point of sale (POS) systems such as credit card swiping devices and, in some instances, cash registers at check-out counters. This malware, referred to as a "RAM scraper," intercepts the information on the card's magnetic strip in the brief moment before the data is encrypted and then transmits the information to the hacker. This type of malware is presently being sold to identity thieves on the black market for as little as $1,000 or as much as $6,000 for more advanced editions of the malware, which must then be downloaded onto the company's computer system, most often through sophisticated phishing tactics or an insider co-conspirator. Presently, retailers do not have security software capable of preventing such attacks; they can only attempt to identify the attack as soon as possible in order to then take the steps to remove the malware. Although Target has gotten most of the publicity for its attack, smaller retailers with less sophisticated systems are probably more at risk and, in fact, might already have had their security breached, but not yet recognized the attack.

So what does this mean to you?

Hotels

White Lodging Services Corporation, which is a company that manages 168 hotel franchises including Marriott, Hilton, and Starwood hotels in 21 states, was hacked in 2014, losing credit and debit card numbers of its customers to identity thieves.

Yahoo E-mail Data Breach

In 2014, Yahoo's e-mail system suffered a data breach. Yahoo is the second-largest e-mail provider, with approximately 273 million users. The actual breach, which involved the theft of both usernames and passwords, was accomplished not by hacking Yahoo directly, but rather by hacking a third-party website's database that allowed the use of Yahoo e-mail addresses to establish customer accounts. Many people might not be particularly alarmed because all that was taken in the Yahoo hacking were usernames and passwords; however, because people often use the same username and password for multiple accounts, including online banking, the threat posed by this hacking could be quite serious. In addition, these usernames and passwords could be used by identity thieves for spear phishing.

Medical Records

Medical records have been fertile ground for identity thieves as more and more patients' records have been maintained electronically. However, the medical industry has been extremely lax in maintaining the security of those records, and because generally medical records contain names, addresses, and Social Security numbers, they represent easy pickings for identity thieves.

In the past three years alone, it has been estimated that 15 million patient records have been stolen, lost, or mishandled.

In 2011, the medical records of five million members of the armed forces were stolen when an employee of Science Applications International Corp (SAIC) left them in his car, which was stolen. The records contained not only medical data, but also Social Security numbers, addresses, and phone numbers.

The private medical records of 20,000 emergency room patients of the Stanford University Hospital were posted on a public website for more than a year before it was noted and stopped. According to Stanford, the information had been sent securely to a data collection service that, in turn, forwarded the information to a company to prepare a graphic presentation of the data. An employee of that company improperly posted the information on a public website as an attachment to a question dealing with converting data into a bar graph. The breakdown of security in this instance is both inexcusable and predictable.

South Shore Hospital in South Weymouth, Massachusetts, had a data breach of the records of 800,000 patients, employees, volunteers, and vendors with which the hospital did business. The hospital blamed an outside data management company for mishandling the records.

In 2012, Eastern European identity thieves exploited security flaws in the Utah Department of Health records. This resulted in data including names, addresses, birth dates, and Social Security numbers of up to 780,000 people being compromised and stolen, thus placing these people in extreme danger of identity theft.

Many of these records were of children, which made them even more valuable to identity thieves due to the fact that identity theft of children is often not discovered for many years because their records are not regularly monitored.

Blame the Employees

Although it is easy to blame the corporate and government officials who are charged with protecting the security of data, identity thieves often target the weakest links, which often are the employees. When employees use company computers to click on tainted attachments in e-mails from hackers, they welcome the malware into their company's computers. Offers of games, music, or pornography have often been the luring culprit for employees who have not given sufficient thought to the dangers of downloading anything from someone of whom they are not sure.

Employees might also take home unencrypted data on their laptops, which they might lose. Here, it is certainly the company's fault, however, for not encrypting the data and for not having better security measures in place.

And sometimes it is a rogue employee with access to information who is the source of a data breach.

Google Dorking

Google is one of the most extremely popular websites on the Internet, full of features, many of which are hardly used by most people. However, unwittingly, Google's advanced search functions have made the lives of identity thieves easier. In 2011, 43,000 staff, faculty, students, and alumni of Yale University had their names and Social Security numbers stolen through the use of Google's FTP search tool that permits unprotected file transfer protocol servers to be accessed. The search for vulnerable information using Google has come to be known as dorking. More than 300,000 people who had filed workers' compensation claims in California had their names, addresses, dates of birth, and Social Security numbers stolen using the same technology. In both instances the files were neither encrypted nor password protected, which would have been simple ways to protect these people from the dangers of identity theft.

Homeland Security Data Breach

It was somewhat distressing in 2013 to learn that the Department of Homeland Security (DHS) had suffered another (yes, I did say another) data breach. The 2013 data breach at the DHS affected thousands of employees of the DHS going back all the way to 2009. The breach of data included the names of employees, their Social Security numbers, and their dates of birth. This is exactly the type of information that is desired by identity thieves because it can readily be turned into identity theft of the people whose data is stolen. The 2013 data breach involved records of a third-party vendor who works with the DHS; however, that is of little comfort to the DHS employees and potential victims of identity theft. In fact, according to a report by the Government Accountability Office (GAO), federal agencies reported more than 25,000 data breaches in 2013, which was double the number of data breaches reported in 2009. It should also be noted that these are just the data breaches that have been discovered. Others are undoubtedly going on undiscovered at this time.

So what does this mean to you and what can you do about this? This data breach points out again, as recognized in the GAO report, that both government and the private sector are still not doing enough to keep our personal information secure. Hopefully this will change, but in the meantime you should limit, as much as possible, the personal information that you provide to both governmental agencies and private companies. In many instances you must provide personal information, but in other situations you can limit the amount of information you provide. For instance, many medical care providers ask for your Social Security number but do not need it. In that instance, you can provide another identifying number, such as your driver's license. You also should consider putting a credit freeze on your credit report, which will prevent an identity thief, who might get access to your Social Security number or other personal information about you, from getting access to your credit report for the purposes of making large purchases.

Data Breaches at Small Businesses

In its 2013 Data Breach Investigations Report, Verizon analyzed data breaches around the world and found that hackers in foreign countries, particularly China, Romania, Bulgaria, and Russia, are responsible for many of the attacks on businesses large and small resulting in data breaches. Sometimes the hacks are intended to obtain company secrets, whereas other times the goal is personal information about a company's customers that can be used to make the customers victims of identity theft. More and more hackers are targeting small businesses both because they are a treasure-trove of information and because many of these companies have lax security, making them easy targets for the hackers. It has been estimated that as much as 80 percent of the data breaches could be prevented if companies were to use two-factor authentication for accessing company computers and their data. This is not a costly security measure to implement, but most companies still do not do this.

Experian Data Breach

In one of the largest data breaches of all time, a sole Vietnamese individual, Hieu Minh Ngo, posing as a private investigator, contacted Court Ventures, a company that is a subsidiary of one of the three major data brokers and credit-reporting bureaus, Experian, and tricked them into providing him with access to the personal and financial records of 200 million Americans. Ngo used this information to provide an illegal service by which he sold this data to identity thieves. Between 2007 and 2013, he provided sensitive personal information including Social Security numbers, dates of birth, and other data to 1,300 identity thieves, whom he charged $1.9 million.

Protecting Yourself from Identity Theft Due to Hacking of a Company or an Agency with Which You Do Business

Although nothing you can do can totally protect you from becoming a victim of a data breach at a company or agency with which you do business, you can take steps to help prevent you from becoming a victim of identity theft if your personal information is compromised through a data breach:

- Use antivirus and anti-malware software security programs and make sure that you keep them current with the latest updates. It is an unfortunate fact that security software is only 5 percent effective in protecting you from the latest viruses and malware. It generally takes about a month for the security software companies to catch up with a patch.

- Limit as much as possible the personal information you provide to the companies and agencies with which you deal.

- Use secure passwords that are difficult to guess and use different passwords for all of your online accounts. Change them regularly.

- Keep backup documentation in case your records at your bank, brokerage house, or any other place that holds your assets are hacked or lost. Copy them regularly to a thumb drive and keep the thumb drive in a secure place in your home.

What to Do If a Company You Do Business With Is Hacked

If a company with which you do business does suffer a data breach, it is important to immediately take the following steps:

- If the hacking involves a credit card, get a new credit card number.

- If the hacking involves a debit card, close the account and get a new bank account and debit card number. Consider limiting your debit card use to ATMs because the laws pertaining to fraudulent use of debit cards are much less consumer-friendly than those for fraudulent use of credit cards.

- Do a credit freeze on your credit report.

- Monitor your credit report every four months using your right to a free credit report annually from each of the three major credit-reporting agencies, by getting one from a different one of them every four months.

- Be aware of identity thieves who will take the opportunity to use spear phishing to contact you for further information under the guise of assisting you following the breach.

9

Identity Theft After Death

I t is interesting to note that a tool for combating fraud and identity theft is used perhaps even more effectively by identity thieves to perpetrate fraud and identity theft. That tool is the Death Master File, which sounds like something Darth Vader would have. Instead, it is a database of information on more than 89 million people. The records contain the name, Social Security number, date of birth, date of death, and ZIP Code of the last residence for people who have died in America since the database's inception in 1980.

The Death Master File was first set up in response to a lawsuit filed pursuant to the Freedom of Information Act. The federal government sells the list and it can be found available, often free, from many different websites.

For years, pranksters still holding a grudge against former President Richard Nixon have used his Social Security number whenever they are required to provide a Social Security number but do not want to cooperate. To check this out, I went to the Death Master File and found that the number floating around on the Internet, 567-68-0515, was indeed correct. However, I certainly do not advise anyone to use this number for any purpose. To do so would be illegal.

The Death Master File is available for insurance companies and various governmental agencies to confirm the death of people to avoid fraud when people might be claiming benefits for someone who has already died. It also can be used by credit card companies to verify that someone applying for credit is not using the identity of someone who has died. Too bad the credit card companies don't actually do that.

However, identity thieves regularly check the list after getting names from obituaries and get the Social Security numbers for recently deceased people. They then access credit in the names of the deceased, as well as file phony income tax returns on behalf of the deceased. When Congress finally was able to reach a budget agreement and stop the federal shutdown in early 2014, a part of the new budget law included removing public access to the Death Master File. However, the list is still available to anyone, including identity thieves, because the National Technical Information Service, the federal agency that manages the Death Master List, still has not closed it because it still needs to make provisions for access to the list by organizations that need the information for legitimate purposes. Meanwhile, a recent study by the federal government's General Accountability Office indicates that some federal agencies that need this information to prevent fraud are not getting the access they need.

Identity theft from the dead has the potential to be more long lasting than other types of identity theft because the victim is dead and others are less likely to notice unauthorized charges or abuse of the person's credit report.

Death Master File and Identity Theft of Children

The Social Security numbers of young children are a particularly sought-after commodity. Social Security numbers for deceased children are perhaps the most valuable of all because of the opportunity for more continued abuse of the identity.

Logan Bryant

It was devastating for the parents of Logan Bryant when their newborn son died of Sudden Infant Death Syndrome (SIDS) at day care, but soon thereafter they faced another blow. Shortly after his death, Logan became a victim of identity theft. Using the Death Master File, identity thieves were able to access Logan's name, birth date, and Social Security number. They were then able to use that information to file a phony income tax return in Logan's name, making him a victim of income tax identity theft.

TIP

Identity theft from dead people is a significant problem, but there are steps you can take to limit this as a problem in your own family. First, you should consider limiting the personal information that you put into a family member's obituary. Often this information is exploited by identity thieves to assist them in making your deceased family member a victim of identity theft. Additionally, you should contact the three major credit-reporting bureaus, Equifax, Experian, and TransUnion, to inform them of the death of your family member and to instruct them to close the credit report of your family member in order to avoid someone with access to your family member's Social Security number from getting access to his or her credit report to use to make large purchases. Although infants do not have credit reports, their deaths do appear in the Death Master File. Hopefully the National Technical Information Service will act soon to prevent this type of identity theft from continuing to happen, and parents, such as those of Logan Bryant, can be spared this extra grief.

Contacting the Credit-Reporting Agencies

A person's credit report is not automatically sealed when that person dies because the credit-reporting agencies do not automatically receive notice that the person has died. Therefore, the first thing that the deceased's personal representative should do is contact the credit-reporting agencies and ask that they lock the account by noting on it that the person is deceased and no further credit should be issued. To accomplish this task, you will need to notify each of the credit-reporting agencies and include the following supporting documentation:

- Copy of appointment as executor or personal representative of the estate of the deceased
- Certified copy of the death certificate
- Name of the deceased
- Date of birth of the deceased
- Social Security number of the deceased
- Most recent address of the deceased
- Request that the file be designated "deceased—do not issue credit"

You should also request a copy of the deceased person's most recent credit report to identify active accounts, which you should then contact in order to close the accounts. In addition to closing all open accounts of the deceased person, you should notify the Social Security Administration, insurance companies, the Department of Motor Vehicles, and the Veteran's Administration if the person was a veteran. You should also notify any organization where the deceased person was a member, such as the public library or gym.

An actual credit freeze should not be required because this will serve the same purpose. You should also contact all companies or governmental agencies with which the deceased had financial dealings to make sure that they are aware of the death and that they know not to issue any further credit.

10

Identity Theft from Children

A study done by Carnegie Mellon CyLab found that the incidence of identity theft was 51 times greater for children than for adults. The Federal Trade Commission estimated that between 2003 and 2011 child identity theft increased more than 300 percent.

Why Would Anyone Want to Steal the Identity of a Child?

Why would anyone want to steal the identity of a child? At first, it would seem that being able to access the credit of a child would not be particularly valuable to an identity thief; however, the truth is that identity theft from children is growing tremendously and with good reason—it pays.

When an identity thief steals the Social Security number of a child, the identity thief can be fairly confident that it is a clean slate. Most parents obtain a Social Security number for their children soon after birth. Without a Social Security number for the newborn, the parents cannot claim the child as a dependent on their income tax returns or obtain medical coverage for the child. It also is much simpler to obtain a Social Security number for a child before the child's first birthday. For all these reasons, most children have Social Security numbers obtained on their behalf shortly after birth.

The identity thief who steals the Social Security number and identity of someone with terrible credit and a horrible credit score on his or her credit report will end up stealing junk. However, stealing a child's identity generally means that there is no credit report. No credit report is certainly not a good credit report, but it is much easier to make profitable than a bad credit report.

What many identity thieves who steal the identities of children do is set up an account with a utility company or a cellphone provider and use a phony name, a phony birth date, and the stolen Social Security number. The identity thief then uses cash to pay for the service. The utility company is not able to provide a credit report for the name and Social Security number used because none exists—that is, until now. However, the company is not concerned with the lack of credit because they have received a cash payment. That first account obtained with the identity thief's phony name and information joined with the child's stolen Social Security number forms the basis for a new, clean credit report in the identity thief's phony name. At this point the identity thief, like a Ponzi schemer, builds up good credit in the credit report by taking out and paying loans and otherwise using credit to sufficiently build up the credit. At that point the thief cashes out by getting a large loan or credit purchase and then disappears, leaving the child's Social Security number tainted. Often a child does not find out about the identity theft until he or she applies for credit, a scholarship, or an educational loan, at which time the damage can be considerable.

Credit-reporting agencies do not intentionally create credit reports for children under the age of 18. However, when they receive data from someone such as a lender or a utility company to be incorporated into a credit report, the credit-reporting agencies do not cross-check the name and age associated with the person's Social Security number with the Social Security Administration to confirm either the age of the person or whether the Social Security number truly matches that name.

Additionally, identity theft from children is used for illegal immigration purposes, such as to provide a clean Social Security number for employment purposes. Also, organized crime uses identity theft from children to do large-scale financial fraud.

How Do You Protect Your Child from Identity Theft?

Just as you should check your own credit report each year by exercising your right to a free credit report from each of the three major credit-reporting agencies, so should you exercise the same right to a free credit report on behalf of your children. Hopefully, nothing will come up under the child's name and Social Security number.

Make sure that you keep your child's Social Security number secure and private. Much identity theft from children comes from family members, baby sitters, or people who have easy access to your home.

Parents can also check with the Social Security Administration on an annual basis to make sure that their child's Social Security number is not being misused.

AllClear ID (www.allclearid.com), a security company, provides a free service called ChildScan, which not only searches credit records tied to your child's Social Security number, but also checks employment records, criminal records, and medical accounts to recognize at an early stage if your child has become a victim of identity theft.

Teach Your Children Well

There are a few things you should impress upon your children for their own safety and to make them less likely to become victims of identity theft:

- For children old enough to use a computer, make sure that they do not provide information on social networking sites that can lead to identity theft. This means they should avoid putting personal information such as addresses and phone numbers online.

- Many parents teach their children how to fish. They should also instruct their children about phishing and how to avoid it.

- Parents should instruct their children to avoid downloading free games and music because this is where keystroke-logging malware might be hiding that can steal all the information stored on your computer.

And, of course, keep your computer security software up-to-date.

RockYou

In 2012, the operators of the online children's game site RockYou settled a claim of the Federal Trade Commission that it did not properly protect the privacy of its users and failed to use proper security, resulting in the site being hacked and the information on 32 million users being compromised. This particular website, by being aimed at children, also violated the Children's Online Privacy Protection Act (COPPA), which requires website operators to notify parents and get their consent before collecting, using, or disclosing personal information from people under the age of 13.

In accordance with the terms of the settlement, RockYou was required to install a new security system and pay a $250,000 fine. As is typical in such FTC settlements, RockYou did not admit that it did anything wrong but promised not to do it again.

Child Identity Theft and Credit-Repair Companies

Credit-repair companies tout their services throughout the media. Some of the less reputable companies will provide you with a new credit identity for credit purposes so that you can avoid the bad credit associated with your own credit report that utilizes your Social Security number. Despite the fact that these advertisements appear in legitimate print and electronic media, they are not screened by the media that accept their advertising dollars, and they are not endorsed by the media in which they appear.

In many instances the clean new credit identity that these companies provide you with is nothing more than a child's stolen Social Security number. Don't be tempted to fall for this scheme. Misrepresenting your Social Security number in a credit or loan application is a crime.

Protecting Your Child's Identity at School

Many school forms ask for personal information about your child. This information, if not properly secured and managed, can result in child identity theft. Fortunately, Congress enacted the Family Educational Rights Privacy Act (FERPA), which helps protect the privacy of student records and provides parents with the ability to opt out of sharing contact information with third parties.

As a prudent parent, you should take certain steps to help prevent your child's identity from being stolen at school:

- Ask the school who has access to your child's personal information.
- Ask the school what security precautions are taken to protect that information.
- When you receive communications from the school asking for personal information about your child, always make sure that you know who will have access to this information and whether you can opt out of the sharing of this information.
- Carefully read the FERPA notice that the school must provide you so that you are aware of your rights to see your child's educational records, to consent to the disclosure of information contained in your child's records, and to be able to correct errors in the school records.
- Many schools maintain a student directory that can contain your child's name, address, date of birth, telephone number, e-mail address, and photograph. Schools are required by FERPA to inform you of their policy as to their student directory, and, most important, the school must inform you of the right to opt out of the release of that information to any third parties. It is a good idea to opt out of such information sharing. The more places that have your child's information, the greater the risk of identity theft.
- Make sure that if your child participates in a program at school that is not sponsored by the school, you are aware of the privacy policy of such after-school programs, such as sports or music programs.

What to Do If Your Child Becomes a Victim of Identity Theft

If, despite your best efforts, your child does become a victim of identity theft, there are two major actions you should take:

- Contact each of the three credit-reporting bureaus and ask them to remove all false information and inquiries fraudulently associated with your child's name or Social Security number. Also send them a copy of the uniform Minor's Status Declaration that explains that the child is a minor.
- Put a credit freeze on the account.

What Can the Government Do?

In 2012, Maryland became the first state to enact a law enabling parents to do a credit freeze on behalf of their children. Before this law was passed, Maryland law required credit-reporting agencies to do a credit freeze for anyone who requested it, but companies could refuse to freeze the credit of anyone who did not already have an account. This created a problem because the credit-reporting agencies would not intentionally create an account for someone under the age of 18, so the only way an account could exist would be if the child was already a victim of identity theft. Since Maryland passed its trailblazing law, a handful of other states, including Delaware, Illinois, Oregon, and Utah, have passed similar laws. Hopefully the rest of the states will follow their lead.

Foster children are particularly susceptible to child identity theft. California, Colorado, and Connecticut have laws that require credit checks for foster children before the child leaves state custody. In 2011, Los Angeles County discovered that 5 percent of its foster children between the ages of 16 and 17 already had credit reports in violation of the policies of all three major credit-reporting agencies. Maryland, however, was the first state to pass a law to help protect the identity of children who were not foster children.

11

Identity Theft Risks of Smartphones and Other Mobile Devices

What you don't know definitely can hurt you. Even people who are extremely security-conscious and careful when using their home computers often fail to consider taking the same security precautions when using their smartphones and other portable electronic devices despite the fact that many of us keep pictures (are you listening, Scarlett Johansson), financial data, passwords, credit card information, and other personal information on our smartphones, iPads, and other portable devices. A report in 2014 by Javelin Strategy & Research found that fewer than 50 percent of people protected their smartphones with security software.

TIP

Although it probably is obvious, it is worth noting that you should never take a picture with your cellphone that you don't want the world to see and either send it to someone or leave it on your cellphone. This lesson was learned the hard way by actresses Mila Kunis and Scarlett Johansson, as well as singer Christina Aguilera, all of whom took nude pictures of themselves that ended up on the Internet when their smartphones were hacked by Christopher Chaney.

Identity thieves are constantly exploiting our lack of appreciation of the severity of the threats posed by the unsecure use of our smartphones and other portable devices. In 2009, a single hacker was able to obtain the e-mails of 145,000 BlackBerry users and forwarded all their e-mails to his location in the United Arab Emirates.

Smartphones make you vulnerable in obvious ways, such as when your cellphone that is not password protected is lost or stolen, and in less obvious ways, such as when the auto-answer feature is hacked, which then allows a hacking identity thief to listen to and record everything that you say on your device. This is accomplished by hacking into the smartphone's baseband processor, which is the mechanism by which radio signals are sent and received on your cellular network, by taking advantage of flaws in the radio chips.

Bluetooth Risks

Using a Bluetooth hands-free connection to your cellphone is advantageous on many levels. It avoids cancer concerns about radiation emanating from the smartphone when it is held directly against the head. It also is safer to use for speaking while driving so that you can have two hands on the wheel, although many safety experts say that merely talking while driving is a safety risk due to the distraction. Unfortunately, Bluetooth hacking is easily accomplished, enabling a hacker to obtain access to the information in your smartphone. However, by having the proper security software on your smartphone and constantly updating it with the latest security patches, you can operate your smartphone with a level of confidence.

Wi-Fi

Many people take advantage of Wi-Fi provided at airports, restaurants, and coffee shops. Although some of these people are aware of the security risks posed to their laptops and take the steps to make sure that they protect those devices with proper security software and mindful use, once again, people tend to be less aware of the risks posed to their smartphones and other portable devices. The danger comes through fake Wi-Fi set up by a nearby identity thief who takes advantage of those who connect to the fake system by stealing the personal information from their smartphones and installing malware permanently on their devices.

4G Systems Vulnerable

Faster smartphone service is a selling point for today's smartphones. The new 4G technology can be up to 100 times faster than 3G networks, and that sounds like a good thing. And it is—for both you and identity thieves. The 4G technology, which is also known as LTE technology, was specifically designed to provide the fast sending and receiving of data; it was not designed for security purposes. The 3G networks use an SS7 protocol for sending signals. This protocol is difficult to hack, whereas LTE networks are faster and can handle more traffic than SS7 networks but are easier to hack.

Until 4G networks are made safer, you might want to stay with a 3G network for more secure use of your smartphone. Regardless of what network you use, you should make sure that you have installed good antivirus software and anti-malware software as well as encryption software. Also, make sure that you keep your security software constantly updated with the latest patches. When choosing a new phone, always do your research as to which phone will provide you with the best security.

SIM Card Danger

Mobile SIM cards are small pieces found in smartphones that enable operators to identify and authenticate a subscriber as they use a particular network. These SIM cards are found in all smartphones regardless of the brand or the technology. Often people store information such as banking information and credit card numbers on their smartphone in the SIM. Access to this information is a gold mine to hackers and identity thieves. Unfortunately, according to Berlin's Security Research Labs, identity thieves are now able to hack into SIM cards using older technology and capture information from these defective SIM cards, which is resulting in identity theft. According to Security Research Labs, more than 500 million smartphones worldwide still use the vulnerable older SIM cards.

The best thing you can do is to contact your smartphone provider to find out whether your phone still uses the older, vulnerable SIM cards and, if it does, replace it with a new phone or a new SIM card.

CRITICAL TIP

It is important to remember that even if you have a PIN for your phone, as I hope you do, a person who steals your smartphone can gain access to important personal information of yours by merely removing the SIM card from your smartphone and putting it into another phone, from which the thief can then readily get your information and use it to make you a victim of identity theft. You can avoid this problem by installing a PIN for the SIM card, which can be done by going to your phone's Settings section.

Even Paranoids Have Enemies

Researchers in London have developed new software called "Snoopy" that can be used with a drone to steal information from your smartphone that can turn you into a victim of identity theft. Although it sounds like something out of science fiction, the idea is simple. It started with a recent federal court decision permitting commercial drones to fly in U.S. airspace. The Snoopy software can be installed on a drone, which can fly around the area where you are and pick up your smartphone's attempt to find a close Wi-Fi network. Snoopy picks up the signal from the smartphone and poses as one of those Wi-Fi connections. After you have unwittingly connected to what appears to be a safe Wi-Fi network, Snoopy is able to steal information from your connected smartphone and use it to make you a victim of identity theft.

Although hackers in America have not yet jumped on this technology, you can expect it to be happening soon. The best course of action for smartphone users and anyone connecting to a Wi-Fi network remains the same as always. Have encryption software on your smartphone or other electronic devices, and also make sure that you install antivirus software and anti-malware software on all of your electronic devices and keep these programs up-to-date with the latest security patches. Finally, only use Wi-Fi networks that you know are legitimate and secure.

Smartphone Charging

Wherever there is a need, some enterprising person will rise to the occasion and come up with a solution. We all have become dependent on our smartphones, tablets, and other portable devices, particularly when traveling. But what if the battery is running low? That could be a problem. Fortunately, wherever you are while traveling, you will be able to find places where you can recharge your smartphone or portable device's batteries. Kiosks in airports and hotels that provide this service are commonplace. There is only one problem: Some of these recharging kiosks are set up by identity thieves who, along with recharging your batteries, steal all the information from your smartphone or other portable device and make you a victim of identity theft.

The safest thing to do is to avoid these kiosks and use your own charger to keep your smartphone or other device fully charged. If that is not possible, you should at least speak to someone involved with security at the hotel, airport, or other venue where the kiosk is found to confirm that it is legitimate. Additionally, you should make sure that all the data in your smartphone or portable device is encrypted and that your smartphone or portable device is protected with the latest security software and that the software is kept up-to-date. Trust me, you can't trust anyone.

Pornography and Smartphones

Identity thieves know that luring people to download free music, games, and, quite often, pornography is a good way to get their victims to download malware such as keystroke-logging programs that can read all the information from your computer and use that information to make you a victim of identity theft. In one famous case, a Florida police officer who was searching for pornography while on his work computer, which, by the way, is a common activity for people at work, unwittingly downloaded a keystroke-logging malware program that enabled the identity thieves to get access to data banks used by police departments, which in turn led to the identity theft of hundreds of thousands of people. Blue Coat's 2013 Mobile Malware Report shows that 20 percent of the time smartphone users went to malicious websites, they were in search of pornography. Fortunately, people are getting a bit savvier when it comes to computer security and are installing security software to help in the battle against malware. Unfortunately, although people are spending more and more time on their smartphones and other portable devices, many people don't even protect these devices with passwords, and too few people protect their smartphones and other portable devices with proper security software and keep it up-to-date.

It is a simple mind-set to make sure that you consider security whenever you are on any electronic device, whether it be a computer, a laptop, a smartphone, a tablet, or any other device. People should also be wary of public Wi-Fi systems, which can be used to steal information from your smartphone or other portable device if you do not have proper security software and encryption programs.

Dangerous Apps

Apps are part of the fun of having a smartphone. They can be utilitarian apps such as calendars or they can be more in the realm of fun and games. Identity thieves know about our love of apps. They also know that people like free stuff. So offering free apps that look like fun is a common identity theft tactic. Often free games and other apps are corrupted with malware that can make your smartphone's data totally within the control of the identity thief. Always check out the legitimacy of an app before you download it. Even more risky is the legitimate app that gets downloaded by the identity thief, who then inserts malware into it and then offers it elsewhere under a confusingly similar name. So always check the ratings on apps and do your own research as to who is behind the particular app. Download apps only from legitimate places such as Apple's App Store or Google's Android Market. Install antivirus security software on your smartphone before you download any apps.

When you do download an app, you will be presented with a list of permissions for services granting access to your hardware and its software, such as your contact list. If the permissions don't make sense, such as a game having you give permission to transmit data from your smartphone, don't complete the download of the app. Certainly any app that wants permission to connect to the Internet or to disclose your identity and location should be treated extremely skeptically. The Google Android Market, Microsoft Windows Phone Marketplace, Research in Motion BlackBerry App World, and the Appstore for Android on Amazon.com all prominently disclose the permissions requested by the apps they sell. The Apple iTunes Store does not disclose such information, so you should always carefully review the requested permissions of any apps you download from the Apple iTunes Store. Apple does say, however, that it does not disclose this information because it has already investigated all the apps that it sells to confirm that they are legitimate, and so far they have done a good job in this area.

Always check your smartphone bill carefully each month because this is where you might first learn that you have downloaded an app that could be stealing money from you, such as when the malicious app makes costly calls or text messages to foreign telephone numbers for which you get billed. These calls can be made from your smartphone without your even being aware of it. You also might find yourself being automatically billed each month for a ringtone or some other service that you did not realize you downloaded at a hidden cost.

Hacking into smartphones is on the rise. It is estimated by Kaspersky Labs, a security company, that the number of hacking attempts went up from 40,059 examples of malicious code in 2012 to almost 100,000 in 2013 created to steal smartphone data, with almost 98 percent of this malicious code aimed at Android devices. Android is the most prominent mobile operating system in the world and is used to power some of the most popular smartphones, such as the Samsung Galaxy. Anything popular with many people is also popular with identity thieves, who look for where the most potential victims are and then focus their efforts on exploiting vulnerabilities in popular software systems. However, another reason Android phones are more at risk for hacking is that unlike the Windows system and iOS systems used on other phones, the Android system is unregulated, which means that anyone can use the code from the Android system to develop apps. More than 98 percent of the malware targeting banking apps was focused on the Android system in 2013 and this hacking is a growth industry. In 2012, there were only 64 malware programs attacking Android banking apps, but by the end of 2013 that number had risen, according to Kaspersky Labs, to 1,321.

Part of the problem with Android systems is that older smartphones are not equipped to operate the latest versions of the Android system, which have incorporated numerous security updates. A particular area of vulnerability in smartphones is malicious apps. Malicious apps that you unwittingly download could include keystroke-logging malware that can steal all the information from your smartphone and use that information to make you a victim of identity theft.

Limit your downloading of apps to well-known, legitimate vendors, such as Google Play. Google scans all apps before it adds them to the Google Play store to make sure that they are not infected with malware. Android apps can readily be found and downloaded to your Android smartphone from multiple sources. Unfortunately, these other sources from which you might download an Android app might not and often do not have the same security standards as the Google Play store, and you are in greater danger of downloading a malicious app. The popular app Candy Crush Saga was hacked into and malware was inserted into it. The now-malicious version of Candy Crush Saga was then listed on less-security-conscious sites other than Google Play and the Apple Store. When consumers downloaded the game from those less-secure sites, they unwittingly infected their devices with the malware.

You should also protect your smartphone with a strong password, install security software and encryption software, and include anti-malware such as the app Lookout, which for $29.99 per year has a feature that continually scans your other apps for viruses and malware, as well as permitting you to lock your phone remotely or eliminate all of your stored data if your smartphone is lost or stolen.

WhatsApp

WhatsApp is a clever name for a company that created a cross-platform mobile messaging app for your smartphone that allows you to send text messages, photographs, videos, and audio. It works with the systems for the iPhone, BlackBerry, Android, Windows Phone, and Nokia. With more than 300 million people already using WhatsApp, it is not surprising that it has become attractive to scammers seeking to use its popularity as a lure into a scam. A couple of scams involving WhatsApp are presently occurring. One starts with a phony WhatsApp e-mail. If you click on the Play button, you are taken to a malicious website where you are further prompted to update your browser. If you click on the links to update your browser, what you will actually be doing is downloading malware onto your computer, smartphone, or other electronic device that can result in your becoming a victim of identity theft.

Another WhatsApp scam starts when you see an ad on your Facebook page offering an app for you to access WhatsApp on your desktop computer. If you fall for this scam and sign up, you will end up unwittingly providing your friends list to the scammer, who can then target your friends with malicious e-mails that appear to come from you.

TIP

Never click on links to update software until you have confirmed that the prompt to do so is legitimate. In this case, you should contact WhatsApp before considering downloading anything that appears to be prompted by a communication from them. As for the Facebook ad, like many scams, it is riddled with spelling errors and grammatical errors that should immediately tip you off that it is a scam, but again, never click on any link until you have confirmed that it is legitimate.

More App Scams

A particularly insidious scam involves your downloading a popular app such as a video player that is corrupted with malware that can take over your text messaging and, without your being aware of it, start sending text messages to premium addresses that cost you money. In addition, the malware can, without your knowing it, make calls to expensive pay-per-call numbers. It is not until you get your first bill after your smartphone has been infected that you learn about the extra charges. The first step in preventing this type of scam is to download apps only from legitimate app stores, such as Apple's App Store or Google's Play Store. Anytime you download an app from a source you are not sure of, you are taking a chance. However, even when you download an app from Apple's App Store or Google's Play Store, you might find yourself victimized because some of the more creative scammers will release a clean app through the Apple App Store or the Google Play Store, which will check out the app, but later the scammer will send you the malware in an update to your app. The best thing you can do in addition to downloading apps only from legitimate companies is to make sure that you have good, effective security software installed on your smartphone. You do it for your computer and your laptop, so make sure that you do it for your smartphone as well.

So What Should You Do?

Fortunately, you can take a number of relatively simple steps to protect yourself from the risk of identity theft through your smartphone:

- Set a security lockout on your smartphone so that when you are not using it, the information contained within it cannot be accessed by someone who might steal or find your smartphone. You can even use a lockout that automatically occurs after a period of time, such as 15 minutes, which should be long enough for you to use your smartphone each time, but provides you with protection if your smartphone is physically stolen.

- When using a Bluetooth connection, you must authorize the connection; make sure you know with whom you are sharing. Even better, you can make your Bluetooth "Not discoverable," which prevents others from connecting to your smartphone. If you don't use Bluetooth, merely turn off the capability and avoid the problem entirely while also extending your battery life. Spyware is easily installed through Bluetooth connections.

- Blackberries, iPhones, and Androids are susceptible to being hacked through malicious downloadable apps. A malicious app version of the popular "Angry Birds" app was responsible for many smartphones being hacked into and their information stolen. Never download an app unless you are sure it is legitimate. If you are using a banking app from your bank, download it directly from the bank's website to make sure that you are not downloading tainted malware. Apple also does a very good job of checking the apps offered at the Apple App Store for legitimacy.

- You install antivirus security software on your home computer and laptop, so why wouldn't you install it on your smartphone, iPad, or other portable device? Use security software and make sure that you keep it updated constantly. Some of the more commonly used security software programs are offered by Lookout, McAfee, Norton, and AVG. Some of these programs are offered free. Users of Google's Android smartphones who failed to update their devices with the latest version of the Android's operating system became vulnerable to hacking of the information on their phone every time they connected to a network. Hackers are always coming up with new challenges for security, so it is absolutely critical not only that you install security software on your smartphone or other mobile device, but that you keep it continually updated and install all new patches.

- Although it is a pain in the neck, use complex and different passwords for each of your devices.

- Never store confidential, personal information such as your PIN number or Social Security number or credit card numbers on your smartphone or other mobile device. You can't lose what you don't have in your smartphone.

- Make sure your SIM card is up-to-date.

- Download apps only from legitimate places such as Apple's App Store or Google's Android Market.

- Check your smartphone bill carefully each month for indications of malicious apps that might, unknown to you, be adding extra charges to your bill.

Smishing

By now most of us are justifiably skeptical of e-mails from Nigeria telling us that we have just inherited millions of dollars; however, people are still too trusting of phony text messages from identity thieves who use text messages purportedly from our bank or other financial institutions telling us that there has been a security problem with our account and that we need to provide confirming information to keep our accounts active. Wells Fargo, Bank of America, Chase, Citibank, Capital One, and many other financial institutions have all been used in smishing scams. The word "smishing" is a variation of "phishing." Just as phishing occurs when you are tricked into going to a phony website that appears to be legitimate and turning over personal information to identity thieves, smishing is the name for the same type of scam when it originates on your smartphone through an SMS, or Short Message Service, the proper name for a text message.

TIP

These smishing messages can look quite convincing, and often they are written well and take advantage of concern about the security of our accounts. I got such a message once and initially was panicked until I remembered that I did not have an account at the particular bank. If you ever receive such a text message, you can never be sure who is sending it. If you have any concerns that it might be legitimate, merely call your bank or other institution at a number that you know is accurate and inquire.

News of the World Hacking Scandal

The *News of the World* was a prominent tabloid newspaper owned by Rupert Murdoch that went out of business in the wake of a hacking scandal that revealed that the newspaper had routinely hacked into the phones of numerous celebrities, politicians, and crime victims. The manner in which the phones were hacked was amazingly simple and again emphasized how by failing to take basic security steps, we unwittingly are assisting the hackers. What the *News of the World* reporters would do was find out the phone or cellphone number of the targeted person and have one hacker call the person and keep him or her on the phone. While the victim was talking to the first hacker, the second hacker would call the targeted person and go into their voicemail. Because the targeted person was usually negligent and had not changed the PIN number to get into the voicemail, the hacker would put in the default PIN given out by the service provider and they could then listen to any cellphone messages of the targeted person.

The problem of the default PIN has been fixed. Now all networks have different PINs, which you set. Some networks allow you to change your PIN only in a call from your own smartphone to prevent hackers from calling, posing as you, and answering security questions and then being able to change the PIN and get access to your voicemail.

Protecting your voicemail begins with a strong PIN that is not easily guessed by a hacker. You also should have a security question that is difficult for a hacker to guess. Remember, even if you are not a celebrity, you probably have a lot of personal information about you online such that someone could learn your mother's maiden name, where you went to school, or your pet's name. Many people don't recognize the amount of personal information they provide to "friends" on Facebook and other social media. I suggest that you use a nonsensical security question, such as "What is my favorite color?" with the answer "seven." It would be impossible for a hacker to guess and silly enough for you to remember. Protecting the security of your smartphone is even more important today than it was years ago, because we all do so much more on our smartphones and they contain much personal and financial information.

Banking with Your Smartphone or Mobile Device

Banking with your smartphone or mobile device can be both convenient and safe if you take the proper steps. Don't assume that your bank is doing its part to keep your transactions safe. Inquire as to its security system, including its use of a strong firewall. Ask about its history of data breaches. Phones get lost and stolen so make sure that you have a good, strong password for your phone. You might also want to have the bank send you e-mail alerts either whenever funds are withdrawn from your account or whenever amounts withdrawn are over a certain threshold. Malicious keystroke-logging programs that you did not realize you have downloaded can provide an identity thief with all the information he or she needs to empty your account. Be wary of phishing, smishing, and tainted apps.

There doesn't seem to be anything common anymore about common sense, but use yours. Your bank should not be sending you text messages or e-mails asking for your password, account number, or personal information. They already have that information. You can be sure that such a text message is from an identity thief. If you have any questions whatsoever, you can always call your bank at a telephone number you know is accurate, not one contained in the text message.

Ultimately, banking through your smartphone can be quite safe. Your smartphone banking can be tied to your specific smartphone so that even if someone were able to hack your banking data from your smartphone, they would not be able to access your account. Smartphones equipped with GPS can also be used to reduce identity theft; if a credit card tied to the account is used many miles away from the smartphone's location, it can be immediately recognized as being questionable.

Tips for Mobile Banking

Mobile banking can be a safe way to do your banking if you follow these important rules:

- Never download apps from unauthorized sources. The risk of these apps being tainted with malware that could steal banking information from your smartphone or other portable electronic device is just too great. Android users should limit their app downloads to the Google Play Store or Amazon's Appstore.

- Android phone users should utilize a four-digit PIN that locks the device when it is not in use. Designating a PIN is an easy task. Just go to Settings and follow the prompts. If you fail to do this, anyone who steals or finds your smartphone or other portable device could have access to your banking app.

- iPhone, iPad, and iPod users should also designate a PIN, which will then automatically encrypt your e-mail and app communications.

- Android phone users need to go back to Settings and click on the Security and Screen Lock link to set up data encryption for the device. This can be done quickly and simply.

Is it safe to do mobile banking? Yes and no. Hackers are actively attacking mobile banking with malicious apps and other social engineering tactics to get access to your bank accounts. However, most of the successful attempts to hack into smartphones and other portable devices have been in Russia, India, Vietnam, Ukraine, and the UK. Russia, by far, is the country where mobile banking has been most common, with 40 percent of the worldwide mobile bank attacks occurring there. Hackers and identity thieves are an enterprising group, and it can be expected that as more and more people utilize their smartphones and tablets for banking, hackers and identity thieves will be focusing more attention on getting a piece of this action. On the other hand, you are probably safer doing your banking from your mobile devices as compared to doing your banking from your computer because the systems for mobile devices were developed with security in mind, whereas security was more of an add-on in the early development of computer systems.

Quick Response Codes

Quick Response Codes are those black-and-white blocks that look somewhat like a bar code that are becoming quite common in various forms of advertising, particularly in magazines. Quick Response Codes allow access to much more data than a traditional bar code. Each Quick Response Code is able to store 7,089 characters or a URL. They are a terrific new way for advertisers to provide you with much information you might desire about a particular product or service, but they also can link you to phony websites that will download malware that can steal the information from your smartphone and make you a victim of identity theft. Use your own good judgment before scanning a Quick Response Code, and make sure your own security software is working and up-to-date.

Reporting Smartphone Theft

The theft of smartphones and cellphones in general accounts for as much as 40 percent of the robberies in large American cities. The theft of information from unprotected phones that can lead to identity theft has prompted the smartphone industry to come up with a system in which now when your cellphone is lost or stolen you can report the loss to your wireless provider and the device will be rendered unable to be used.

Warning Signs That Your Smartphone Has Been Hacked

Here are a few telltale signs to look for that indicate your smartphone might have been hacked:

- Browsing on your smartphone is slow.
- The battery needs more frequent recharging.
- The call history shows calls that you have not made.
- Charges for services that you have not incurred appear on your phone bill.

Getting Rid of Your Old Smartphone

Most people get a new smartphone about every 18 months, and it is important to make sure that all the information contained on your old smartphone has been deleted. AccessData, a forensic technology company that works with various private companies and government agencies, checked out phones it purchased from various cellphone resellers, including eBay and Craigslist, and found that although the data appeared to be removed, they were still able to retrieve from the phones Social Security numbers, passwords, and other personal financial information that would have put the former cellphone owners in jeopardy of identity theft. AccessData recommends that before disposing of a cellphone, you have a factory reset of the phone done to remove all data.

12

Identity Theft Threats with Credit Cards and Debit Cards

The combination of the fact that everyone has credit cards and debit cards with the fact that they present easy targets for identity thieves has made credit cards and debit cards fertile ground for the efforts of identity thieves. Some of the identity theft scams steal your credit card or debit card information and data through the use of technology, whereas other scams creatively lure you into providing the information to the identity thieves yourself.

Credit Card Liability

The good news is that the maximum liability that you face for fraudulent charges is limited to $50 even if the card is used before you report its misuse. In fact, if the fraudulent charges were made with your credit card number but not your actual card itself, you have no liability whatsoever for its fraudulent use. In addition, many credit card companies waive the $50 charge. The main problem with identity theft through credit cards is the time and effort you must invest in remedying the situation by getting new cards and, perhaps, most time-consuming and difficult, repairing your credit report if the fraudulent charges have turned up on your credit report as bad debts.

Debit Card Liability

Debit card liability for fraudulent charges is limited to $50, but only if you report the loss within 2 business days. If you are not monitoring your account in a timely fashion, the amount you can lose can be dramatically more. If you report the fraudulent charges after 2 days but no later than 60 days after the charges have been incurred, your losses are capped at $500. However, if you do not report the fraudulent charges until after 60 days, there is no limit to the loss from your bank account for fraudulent charges. Some issuers of debit cards will not hold you to these standards; however, even if you report the fraudulent charges immediately, it can take weeks for a bank investigation to be completed and for you to have access to the money stolen from you through the fraudulent charges. If you have written checks based on your correct account balance, those checks could bounce during the investigation period. Debit cards are best used in a limited fashion at ATMs to limit your potential liability. Credit cards are also better for purchases of retail goods because they provide you with protection, if the goods are defective or if you are billed incorrectly, that debit cards do not provide.

IMPORTANT DEBIT CARD TIP

If you prefer not to heed my advice about restricting your debit card's use to ATMs, consider setting up two separate bank accounts. Use one account for your automatic payments, such as your mortgage or car payments, and do not get a debit card for that account. By not using a debit card for that account, you avoid the problem of that account being frozen pending an investigation by your bank if a debit card for that account has been hacked. You can use the other account for ordinary spending, and if the security of your debit card for that account is breached, you do not need to worry about any of your automatically paid bills being late.

Small Charge on Your Credit Card Scam

This particular scam has been around for ten years, but with the increased hacking of credit card information from major retailers, the scam has been increasing in frequency. The scam starts when your credit card number is compromised and falls into the hands of an identity thief. Although this can happen in a myriad of ways, one of the more common ways is that the people who hack large numbers of credit card numbers from companies such as Target sell the numbers to identity thieves on black market websites. Some identity thieves will buy thousands of credit card numbers and then set up phony online businesses from which they make monthly charges on the cards in small amounts, such as $9.84. Why, you might ask, do they use this number? Many people do not scrutinize their monthly credit card statement sufficiently, particularly when the charge is an innocuous amount that is less than $10 and appears to be made to a legitimate-sounding company. Thus, the scam might continue for great periods of time before it is discovered. This scam has been a particular favorite of identity thieves in Cyprus, the UK, and India who have gone to great effort to create websites for phony but legitimate-looking companies from which these charges are made.

To cite a famous quote attributed to a number of early American Revolutionary leaders, including Thomas Jefferson, "The price of liberty is eternal vigilance." That quote is certainly applicable to life today in regard to avoiding scams and identity theft. It is important to review your credit card statements, bank statements, and other account records carefully each month and even more often, online. Identifying any irregularities or improper activities and reporting them immediately is a good way to protect yourself from serious identity theft.

Debit Card Texting Scam

In this scam people receive a call or a text message informing them that the bank account accessible through their debit card is frozen. The potential victim is then given a telephone number to call to straighten out the matter. The number is, of course, phony and not tied to any bank. If the number is called, the potential victim can be turned into a real victim if they provide the personal information asked for by the identity thief, who then uses the information to access the victim's bank account.

If you receive such a call or text message, you should ignore it. Many people have received calls purporting to be from banks where the people receiving the calls don't even have bank accounts. This happened to me. Never provide information to anyone who calls or texts you because you can never be sure who they are. Even if you have Caller ID that indicates that the call is from a legitimate source, you cannot trust the call because Caller ID can be fooled into showing what appears to be a legitimate call through a technique called spoofing. If you are concerned that the call might not be legitimate, merely call your bank at a number that you know is legitimate, and you will soon learn whether the original call or text was phony.

Mobile Payment Technology

In an effort to make using credit cards easier, the no-swipe credit card, sometimes referred to as the mobile wallet, was developed. These cards use radio frequency identification chips to provide for the use of the card without its having to be swiped through a processing terminal. To use your no-swipe credit card, all you have to do is to wave the card by a terminal that will read the card and transmit your purchase data. Easy and convenient. However, despite the assurances of the issuers of these cards that the information is encrypted and therefore protected, the fact is that not all issuers of these cards are encrypting the data on the card. The cards therefore could be easily readable by an identity thief with a pocket-size portable device who, by merely walking near you, can read the card through your wallet or clothing in an act of electronic pickpocketing. Another way that electronic pickpocketing is accomplished is through the downloading of apps that appear to be for games or some other legitimate use that are corrupted with malware that will, when the smartphone is placed close to the credit card, as in a woman's purse or a man's pocket, scan the card and send the information to the identity thief far away.

Pinellas County Florida Sheriff's Detective Korey Diener has said that in recent years, stealing of information from smart cards that can lead to identity theft has become a problem at malls, sporting events, and other crowded places.

Some enterprising businesspeople have seen an opportunity where others see a problem and have developed metal wallets that can protect the no-swipe cards from walk-by identity thieves. These are a good choice. Some people merely wrap their credit cards in aluminum foil before putting them in their wallet or purse, and this too will effectively block illegal card reading.

According to the Bureau of Justice Statistics' National Crime Victimization Survey, it is predicted that by 2016 a billion of these no-swipe cards will be issued, and unless immediate action is taken by the card issuers to make these cards safer, we are likely to see a huge increase in credit card identity theft.

TIP

If you have a smart card, you should make sure that the issuer of your card encrypts the data on the card to make it even more difficult for an identity thief to get useful information.

Credit Card Technology

The hacking of Target and Neiman Marcus in late 2013 resulting in the theft of credit and debit card information on more than 100 million Target and Neiman Marcus customers brought attention to the technology used in American credit cards. Unlike credit cards in other parts of the world, American credit cards still use a magnetic strip technology that has been around since the 1960s in which information is contained on a magnetic strip on the back of the card. When the information on this strip is stolen, the identity thief has access to the credit of the victim. However, in more than 80 other countries around the world, the magnetic strip card technology has been replaced with cards embedded with a microchip. This technology is often referred to as EMV. With EMV cards, the chip creates and encrypts a new number every time the card is used. Thus hacking into the data terminals used by the cardholder is a worthless exercise in trying to access the credit card. Banks and retailers have resisted calls to update the credit card system in America to the newer EMV cards due to an estimated cost of $8 billion to make the necessary changes to the country's credit cards, debit cards, card terminals, and ATMs. There is little doubt that the change to the newer technology will significantly reduce data breaches and attendant identity theft. When the UK switched to EMV cards, credit card fraud dropped by 34 percent. In Canada the decrease in card fraud was even greater. In the five years since Canada adopted EMV technology, card fraud has gone down 45 percent.

Regulatory changes in regard to liability for fraudulent credit card use will prompt credit card companies and retailers to switch to EMV technology by October of 2015. However, this should not be seen as a panacea because the switch to EMV cards will not reduce online credit card fraud.

ATM Scam

A scam that has been quite successful for identity thieves to get people to reveal their debit card information starts with a text message that purports to be from your bank informing you that your ATM card has been deactivated due to security reasons and that you need to call the telephone number provided to reactivate the card. The text message appears legitimate and it even identifies the account by the first four digits of the card, which gives the text message a greater appearance of legitimacy. Unfortunately, many people are not aware that the first four digits of an ATM card are not distinctive for each card. Instead, they merely indicate the particular bank and its location, which is easy information for any identity thief to obtain. But to an unsuspecting victim, it appears that the bank is merely truncating the number for security reasons as is done on credit card receipts. After the victim responds to the urgent text and calls the telephone number provided in the text, he or she is asked to confirm the full ATM card number and PIN for security reasons. When this information is turned over to the identity thief, the thief is then able to fully access the victim's bank account by creating phony ATM cards using the information provided by the victim.

TIP

Many people know right away that this is a scam when they receive the text message because the texts are sent out in a wide net, including people who don't even have cards at the particular bank. For anyone else who receives such a text, you can never be sure who is sending you that text, so if you have any concerns call the bank by using a telephone number that you know is accurate. By the way, your bank will never ask you for your PIN.

Another Similar Scam

Sometimes, identity thieves have already stolen your credit card number, name, address, and telephone number. But that is not enough for them. They also want the security code numbers on the back of your credit card that are often used for Internet purchases to confirm that you are in possession of the card. They call you and tell you that they are from your card-issuing bank and that there has been a security problem with your card. They confirm your number and tell you that they just need to confirm with you that you still are in possession of the card so they need you to read to them the security numbers on the back of your card. Many people, thinking that the call must be legitimate because the caller already had the credit card number, provide the security code numbers on the back of the card and turn themselves into victims of identity theft.

> **TIP**
>
> You never know who is calling you on the phone. If you receive such a call, regardless of what they tell you, hang up, and if you have any concerns call the bank at a number that you know is correct.

Skimmers

Skimmers are small portable devices that identity thieves can easily obtain that are used to swipe your credit card or debit card and steal the information from the card to make you a victim of identity theft. Sometimes the device is used by a criminal waiter or clerk at a store who swipes your card through the skimmer while processing your card through the legitimate terminal. Some restaurants, to avoid this as a concern, bring over a mini terminal to your table so that your credit card never leaves your sight. It is always a good idea to closely watch your card whenever you present it to a waiter or a clerk, although particularly in restaurants, this is not always possible to do. Sometimes, however, you do the swiping of your card through the skimmer yourself without even knowing it. Skimmers can be and are attached to gas pumps, grocery store checkouts, and ATM machines so that when you swipe your card as you would normally, you are also swiping it through the skimmer. Often when the skimmer is located at an ATM machine, the identity thieves will also install small cameras to view you inputting your PIN number. For this reason it is always a good idea to shield the PIN pad with your other hand as you input your PIN. Some identity thieves even install thin covers over the keypad that will capture your PIN. Skimmers are also available that will even transmit the data electronically to an identity thief, whereas others merely store the data for the identity thief, who returns to retrieve the skimmer. After the data is obtained through the skimmer, phony cards are created by the identity thieves to steal from your credit card or from your bank account using the debit card.

One type of scam used to get your credit card involves both a skimmer to read your card and tampering with the ATM so that it does not work. You might find that a helpful fellow customer will offer to help you get the machine to accept your PIN. This helpful fellow is actually an identity thief who is just using this as an opportunity to get your PIN.

Skimming is big business. It is estimated that losses from skimmers at ATMs total more than a billion dollars each year.

But the use of skimmers is not limited to ATMs. In 2014, 13 people were arrested for identity theft perpetrated through skimmers installed in gas pumps at Raceway and RaceTrac gas stations in Texas, Georgia, and South Carolina. The stolen information was transmitted from the skimmer using Bluetooth technology to the identity thieves, who then made phony credit cards using that data, which they then used to withdraw cash from ATMs in New York City.

Credit Card Processing Companies

A weak link in the credit card process that is being exploited more and more by identity thieves is the credit card processing companies. These are companies, such as Global Payments and Heartland Payment Systems, that work with the major credit card companies and act as the middlemen between retailers and the banks issuing the cards. They process charges between retailers, the credit card companies, and the issuing banks. Identity thieves have been focusing increasing attacks in recent years at payment processors because their security is not as sophisticated as that of the banks. The Federal Deposit Insurance Corporation (FDIC) has been warning about this vulnerability for years. Identity thieves have been targeting these credit card processing companies because they are able to get access to information pertaining to so many credit cards in one place. Heartland Payment Systems was hacked into starting in 2007, and it was not discovered until two years later, resulting in the exposure of data on 140 million credit cards. Global Payments was hacked into twice in 2011 and 2012, resulting in the loss of data on up to three million credit cards.

Those whose cards were compromised were contacted by their card issuers, but it is always better to continually monitor your own monthly statements for any irregularities due to the fact that some of these credit card processing company hacks go on for so long before they are discovered.

Make the Matter Even Worse

Identity thieves see everything as an opportunity. Following the disclosure of the hacking into credit card processing companies, they will contact you posing as your bank or credit card company, offering to help you, but actually just seeking more personal information to make you a victim of identity theft again. Never give personal information to someone you have not contacted and are not totally confident is legitimate.

A Little Defense

Defense, we are told, wins championships. It also can help protect you from becoming a victim of identity theft in regard to your credit and debit cards. Here are some things to keep in mind:

- Pay attention to when you receive your monthly credit card bills. If a credit card bill is late, it could be an indication that your identity has been stolen and the identity thief has changed the address of the account. Contact your credit card issuer as soon as possible if you find that your bill appears to be late.

- When you do receive your monthly credit card statement and bank account statement, review the statements carefully. Some large identity theft rings will test out the credit card or debit card they have access to with small charges to make sure that the account is active, and if the charge goes through, they will then make their larger charges to your account.

- Never use an ATM card in an ATM machine that looks as though it might have been tampered with by the installation of a skimmer. Or if you notice what might appear to be a pin-sized hole on the top of the ATM, it could be concealing a small camera used to view you input your PIN number.

- Cover the keypad with your other hand when you input your PIN to avoid someone or a camera seeing your PIN.

- Be particularly wary of private ATMs as compared to those of major banks. Although these private ATM machines are perfectly legal, they are also more easily purchased by an identity thief, who can merely tamper with the inside of the machine to more readily steal your ATM card information.

- Never carry your PIN number written down in your wallet or purse.

- Some credit card issuers, such as Capital One, provide a service whereby you can receive e-mail or text alerts if your card balance goes up or down by a set amount that you determine. This is a good service to utilize, as is Citibank's system to text you if there is an unusual charge being processed. American Express provides for an alert to you if someone obtains a cash advance on your card. Check and see what types of notification services are provided by your card.

Disputing Fraudulent Charges on Your Credit Card

Although the law limits your liability for unauthorized charges that appear on your credit card to no more than $50, some credit card companies do not even charge you the $50. It is important for you to notify the credit card issuer within 60 days of when the credit card company sent you the bill that shows fraudulent charges as a result of identity theft. It is particularly important to keep track of when you normally receive your monthly credit card bill because an identity thief might have changed the address of your account, so unless you are vigilant it could be several months before you notice that you have not been receiving credit card bills. Direct your letter to the address for billing inquiries shown on your credit card bill. Do not send your letter to the same address to which you normally send your payment. In your letter describe the amount and the date of all fraudulent charges and include a copy of your identity theft report. Send the letter by certified mail return receipt requested so that you will have a good record of having sent the letter. Within 30 days of receiving your letter, the credit card company must send you an acknowledgment of receipt, after which the credit card company must resolve your complaint within two billing cycles or in less than 90 days after getting your letter.

13

Medical Identity Theft

Medical identity theft, as a specific variation of identity theft, is still relatively unknown by the general public, but it may be the most dangerous form of identity theft of all because it not only, as with most forms of identity theft, can affect your finances, but also can affect your health. It can even cause you to receive improper medical treatment due to incorrect information contained in your medical records due to the actions of the medical identity thief. It can also cause you to be dropped by your medical insurance provider or pay an increased premium.

As more and more of our medical records become digitized, the risk of medical identity theft will increase unless the medical community makes more of an effort to protect the privacy and security of these records.

Big Problem

A recent study done by the Ponemon Institute indicates that the extent of the problem is even bigger than previously thought, with more than half of all healthcare organizations reporting medical identity theft. In 2013 there were more than 1.84 million victims of medical identity theft, which represents an increase of 21 percent over 2012. Medical identity theft is often an inside job in which rogue employees steal the health insurance information of patients and sell it to identity thieves. Due to federal HIPAA medical privacy regulations, it is incredibly difficult to have the medical information of a medical identity thief whose information gets intermingled with the victim's medical records removed from the victim's medical records. Medical identity theft is also happening as a result of data breaches of the healthcare providers.

Inquire of your healthcare providers what they are doing to maintain the security of their records, and consider using an alternative healthcare provider if they are not doing enough. Also, carefully check your medical bills when you receive them. Many people only look to see whether they owe anything, and if they do not, they don't bother to carefully check the rest of the bill to makes sure that no inaccurate charges are contained on the bill. Phony charges on your medical insurance can cost you money by eating up your coverage. If you find improper charges, report them immediately to your healthcare provider, and ask that the charges be removed and at a minimum that your medical records identify the records of the identity thief mixed in with yours. If possible, ask that your records be purged of incorrect information.

How It Happens

Medical identity theft begins when your medical insurance records are accessed and then sold to be used to provide medical services to someone else using your insurance. This can harm you in two ways. The first way is that the medical identity thief might incur large medical bills in your name that might not be covered by your medical insurance and collection companies would come after you for the payment. The second way is that these bad debts can have a disastrous effect on your credit report, which in turn can affect your life in so many ways, from getting a job to getting a loan to being able to buy insurance. What is unique about medical identity theft, however, is that the mingling of your medical records with those of the medical identity thief can result in your receiving improper care that can result in dangerous situations, such as your receiving a blood transfusion of the wrong type of blood. You also can run into difficulties in accessing your health insurance as coverage amounts on your policy are used by people other than you, making it more difficult to get the benefits of your own health insurance policy.

Sometimes medical insurance records are obtained by hackers, as was the case when Eastern European identity thieves hacked into the health records of 780,000 people from the Utah Department of Health in 2012. In that case, the identity thieves were able to guess a weak password that failed to protect the information.

Other times the records are obtained by rogue employees who steal the medical information and sell it to professional medical identity thieves. In 2012, an employee of the South Carolina Department of Health and Human Services stole 228,435 Medicaid files, a full 20 percent of all the Medicaid recipients in South Carolina.

Your medical records are maintained by your primary care physician, your pharmacy, your dentist, insurance companies, government agencies, and human resource departments where you work, as well as consultants who work with any of your medical providers, so you are at risk of medical identity theft in many places.

According to a PricewaterhouseCoopers report, digitized health records that have the potential to provide tremendous benefits both in security of records and in treatments are at the present time a significant source of the problem of medical identity theft because too many institutions using digital medical records are not doing enough to encrypt the data, limit access, use proper and complex passwords, and provide for systems to track unauthorized use. According to the PricewaterhouseCoopers report, "The Global State of Security," less than half of the 8,000 healthcare executives surveyed reported that their companies encrypted data, and only 37 percent of these companies had an information security strategy.

Indications That You Are a Victim of Medical Identity Theft

Just as it is important to regularly monitor your financial accounts for indications of identity theft, it is also important to be on the lookout for clues that you have become a victim of medical identity theft. Here are some ways to tell if you have become a victim of medical identity theft:

- An item appears on your insurance Explanation of Benefits form for a service or treatment you did not receive.
- You receive a notice from your insurer that your benefits have reached their limits when you did not incur services that would cause this to happen.
- You are contacted by a debt collector regarding a bill for medical services you did not receive.

What Can You Do to Help Prevent Medical Identity Theft?

Taking the necessary steps to prevent becoming a victim of medical identity theft is the best way to deal with this problem. Here are some things you should be doing:

- Although such statements are often hard to decipher, carefully review all of your medical bills and insurance statements, sometimes called an Explanation of Benefits, even if you are not being required to pay anything, to make sure that your medical insurance is not being used for medical care that you did not receive.

- Just as you should regularly check your credit report, you also should regularly check your medical records to make sure that there are no mistakes, which can be important not only in regard to medical identity theft, but also in ensuring that there are no mistakes that could affect your ability to obtain various types of insurance, such as life insurance or long-term care insurance.

- Many medical insurance companies still use your Social Security number as an identifying number for your health insurance. The worst offender is Medicare. Despite numerous federal studies by the General Accountability Office (GAO), the investigative arm of the federal government, urging Medicare to stop using Social Security numbers as Medicare identification numbers, Medicare refuses to do. You never get what you don't ask for. It is at least worth a try to ask your health insurance company for a different identification number. And while you are at it, although most of us routinely provide our Social Security number to our physicians and other health care providers when asked, there is no reason related to medical care that they need this number. The real reason they ask for it is to make it easier to collect overdue medical bills.

- Read the HIPAA (Health Insurance Portability and Accountability Act) forms that your physicians and treating hospitals ask you to sign. I know that is a difficult task likely to bring on drowsiness, but it is important to do so. Without realizing it you might be giving your physician authority to share your medical information with whomever he or she wants. Always ask with whom your medical information will be shared and what security measures they take to protect the privacy of your records.

- HIPAA provides for you to be able to request from your healthcare providers a free annual Accounting of Disclosure, which is a list of everyone who received your medical information for uses other than treatment or payment within the past year.

- Never give out your medical insurance information or any other medical information on the phone or online to anyone unless you are absolutely sure they are legitimate. Medical identity thieves pose as employees of your insurance company or your doctor. If you have not made the call, don't give the information. You can always call the proper medical provider or insurance company at a number you know is correct.

- Never share your medical information online unless the URL begins with "https" rather than the more common "http." "Https" means that the data is encrypted.

- Shred, shred, shred your old medical records that you have at home that you don't need. Otherwise, dumpster-diving medical identity thieves can go through your trash and turn it into gold.

What Do You Do If You Become a Victim of Medical Identity Theft?

If you discover you have become a victim of medical identity theft, take the following steps:

- If you become a victim of medical identity theft, the law provides for you to get a copy of all of your medical records from your various healthcare providers. Review them carefully to identify any incorrect data. Complete an identity theft report and file a report with the police. After you identify that incorrect data, you have the right to have your records amended. However, this is easier said than done. To have your medical records corrected, you must fill out forms describing the errors. Also send the medical providers a copy of your police report and your identity theft report. Expect the medical providers to take a long time to investigate the matter. Another problem is that due to flaws in HIPAA regulations, some healthcare providers are likely to keep incorrect information in your file and merely note that it is disputed.

- Send copies of your police report and identity theft report to your health insurance company's fraud department and the fraud departments of each of the three credit-reporting bureaus.

- Get an Accounting of Disclosure so that you can identify who received incorrect medical information, and contact them in order to correct their records.

- Put a credit freeze on your credit report. If a medical identity thief has your medical insurance information, the thief is sure to have your Social Security number. By putting a credit freeze on your credit report, you can prevent them from using your identity to make the kind of large purchases that would require the retailer to check out your credit report.

- Check your file with the Medical Information Bureau (MIB). This is the company used by insurance companies to share medical information. Insurance companies use this company to verify medical information before issuing insurance policies, such as life insurance. If you are a victim of medical identity theft, your file might be corrupted with information that could interfere with your ability to get life insurance in the future. The MIB is regulated by the same laws that regulate credit-reporting agencies, so you are entitled to a free copy of your report once a year at no charge. If you find errors, you should request that the MIB investigate and amend your file.

14

Identity Theft and Social Media

Social networking is as much a part of modern life as a morning cup of coffee. Facebook, Twitter, LinkedIn, Pinterest, Instagram, and other social networking sites are the way that most people communicate. With more than 500 million people on Facebook alone, you can expect that scammers and identity thieves will be there, too, taking advantage of every trick in the book to lure you into becoming a victim of identity theft. It is dangerous out there and often we are our own worst enemy. For example, it is common for people, without thinking, to put their vacation travel plans on their Facebook page for the world to see, thus possibly setting themselves up for a burglary. Fortunately, if you know what the danger signals are, you can enjoy social media with less danger of becoming a victim of identity theft.

What Interests You?

Whatever interests you or arouses your curiosity is sure to arouse the interest of identity thieves, who are generally the first to respond to anything in the news, such as a natural disaster or death, as well as gossipy items that people are always interested in. Identity thieves will load keystroke-logging malware onto the links that you might find on your Facebook page. Here are some of the more famous instances in which this occurred:

- Links to secret photos of Osama Bin Laden immediately after his death
- Links to incredible photographs of the natural disasters
- Links to embarrassing videos of Justin Bieber
- Links to compromising videos of Miley Cyrus
- Links to anything Kardashian

Facebook Scams

It is no surprise that just as Facebook is the most popular social networking site with the general public, Facebook is also the favorite social networking site for identity thieves and scammers. Identity theft schemes and scams are always being developed to victimize legitimate Facebook users, and the same scams often reappear after a period of time to take advantage of a new wave of unwary users. Here are some of the more popular scams and identity theft threats found on Facebook:

- A link appears on your wall informing you that Facebook now has a dislike button and that all you need to do is to click on a link to activate this feature. Don't do it. Facebook does not have a dislike button and it is unlikely that it ever will. If you do click on the link, it will install malware on your computer that will permit it to access your profile, post spam, and lure you into completing surveys and providing information that can be used to make you a victim of identity theft. If you fall victim to this scam, delete it from your Facebook account as quickly as possible.

- An offer appears on your Facebook page in which you are told that if you link your debit card to your Facebook account, you will get 20 percent cash back whenever you use the card. This too is phony and after you have provided your debit Visa or MasterCard card information, you have given an identity thief the key to your bank account. If any offer sounds too good to be true, it usually is. If you have any doubts, merely contact Facebook to confirm whether an offer is legitimate.

- A link to an app appears on your wall that says it will let you see who has accessed your profile. Unfortunately, there is no such app and never will be. There is no way of knowing who has viewed your profile. However, when you click on the link, you download keystroke-logging malware that can steal your personal information from your computer and make you a victim of identity theft.

- You receive an e-mail telling you that your Facebook account has been canceled and that you need to click on a link to either confirm or cancel the request. The link doesn't take you to an official Facebook page, but it does take you to a third-party application present on the Facebook platform, which unfortunately fools many people into thinking it is legitimate. If you click on the link, you are asked to allow an unknown Java applet to be installed and you are told that your Adobe Flash must be updated. Unfortunately, if you click to update your Adobe Flash, you are not updating your Adobe Flash, but downloading a keystroke-logging malware program that will steal all your personal information from your computer and make you a victim of identity theft.

- You receive an e-mail that says, "LAST WARNING: Your account is considered to have violated the policies that are considered annoying or insulting to Facebook users." This is a scam and an attempt to obtain information from you that can lead to your identity theft. If you have any concerns, contact Facebook at an address you know is accurate. Also, always be particularly wary when the grammar is poor.

- You receive an e-mail from Facebook telling you that someone is logging into your Facebook account from a device or computer you have not used before. In fact, Facebook will notify you about unauthorized access, but they will never ask you for personal information. Identity thieves always do.

- You receive a message telling you that you have been tagged in a Facebook post. When you go to Facebook and click on the link, you are then directed to a website that prompts you to download either a browser extension or a plug-in in order to be able to watch a video that is alleged to pertain to you. Unfortunately, what you actually are downloading is not a browser extension or a plug-in, but keystroke-logging malware that enables the identity thief who planted it to steal all the information from your computer, including your Social Security number, passwords, credit card information, bank account information, and more. He or she then uses that information to make you a victim of identity theft and make your life miserable. Never click on links unless you are absolutely sure that they are safe. Even if the link or download appears in a Facebook message or e-mail that appears to come from a friend of yours, you can't be sure either whether your friend's account has been hacked or whether your friend, unwittingly, is passing on tainted material. Also, make sure that all of your electronic devices, including your computer, smartphone, and tablets, are protected with security software including anti-malware software and that you keep your security software constantly updated.

Facebook Tips

There is nothing you can do to totally guarantee that you will not become a victim of identity theft; however, there are important and relatively easy steps you can take to protect yourself from identity theft when using Facebook. Don't use your proper name for your account. Don't make it easy for an identity thief to see who you are. Don't list your real birth date. This is another piece of information that can be exploited by an identity thief. Never store your credit card number on Facebook or any other website for convenience. This also makes it quite convenient for an identity thief to access your credit card if he or she hacks into Facebook or your account there. Be careful about the amounts of what might appear to you to be innocuous information on your Facebook page. Some of it can lead to the answers to your security questions on various accounts of yours. Don't befriend everyone who asks. Among those new friends might be identity thieves. Never click on links or downloads from your "friends" unless you have confirmed both that the message containing the link or download actually came from them, as opposed to a hacker who has hijacked their account, and that the material being sent is secure.

From Facebook to Your Bankbook

It is a relatively easy matter for someone to hack into the Facebook account of one of your friends. They then send you a message with a link that you trust because it appears to be coming from one of your friends. The link then takes you to a phony phishing page that appears to be a Facebook login page, where you insert your password to reenter Facebook. You have now turned over your Facebook password to the identity thief. Armed with that, the identity thief then has access to all the information you have input into your own legitimate Facebook page, which often might have the information many of us use as security questions for services such as online banking. Because many people make the mistake of using the same password for everything, you have now provided the identity thief with both your bank account password and information necessary to answer your security question. At that point the identity thief has enough information to empty your bank account.

TIP

Use different passwords for different accounts and change them on a regular basis. When determining security questions, consider whether people would be able to readily access the information necessary to answer your security question from information that might be available online. A good security question has a nonsensical answer, such as "seven" being the answer to the question of what your favorite color is. This is so silly that you will remember it and so illogical that no identity thief will ever guess it. While on Facebook, if a link takes you back to a Facebook log-in page, immediately exit the browser. Do not type your password.

Celebrities and Facebook

Teasing messages, such as the phony "OMG I just hate RIHANNA after watching this video. You will lose all your respect for RIHANNA after watching this" have been used to get people to download malware that ends up stealing the information from their computer and makes them a victim of identity theft.

If you are even tempted to click on that link for those types of photographs or videos, first consider the source. If you don't know the source, don't click on the link. If you think you know the source, confirm the source with a telephone call to make sure that the link is actually from that person. And if a source you know truly did send the link, make sure you do an updated security scan on your computer before you even consider clicking on the link. And then don't click on it. Some security software won't protect you if you click on one of these links to malware because you are going to it through your Facebook application.

Miley Cyrus Sex Video

Curiosity killed the cat, but for us humans, it can too often lead to identity theft, which, although certainly not as bad as death, can be pretty devastating. One such scam periodically appears on Facebook pages where you will find an announcement about a breaking news story regarding a secret sex tape of Miley Cyrus. If you click on the link in order to view the tape, a request for you to prove that you are over 18 appears. When you fill in the information requested, it can not only lead to your identity theft, but also allow the identity thief to steal your Facebook information so that Facebook messages from the scammer/identity thief will appear to be coming from you, which will make your friends more likely to trust the message and end up becoming victims of identity theft themselves. By the way, there is no such sex tape.

Never trust links provided by anyone on your Facebook page or anywhere else without checking out their validity first. Links luring you with promises of sex tapes of Miley Cyrus or nude pictures of princess Kate Middleton, the wife of Prince William (which do actually exist), or anything else that would tempt you to click on the link are an effective way for identity thieves and scammers to trick you into downloading viruses or keystroke-logging malware and make you a victim of identity theft. If you want to check out the veracity of some gossip, a safe place to go is www.tmz.com. And of course, as I always say, "Trust me, you can't trust anyone"—even if you receive e-mails, texts, or Facebook messages from people you trust, you can't be sure that they haven't been hacked, resulting in the message coming from a scammer, and it's also possible that they could be inadvertently passing on tainted links that they don't realize contain a virus.

E-mails

The Nigerian letter is alive, well, and constantly evolving, although the essence is the same. You are contacted about being let in on a tremendous opportunity for great wealth. Whereas the Nigerian letters often dealt with inheritances or getting money out of Nigeria, today's e-mails might entice you into participating in business deals or other opportunities. One that flourished at the time of the death of Moammar Gadhafi was an e-mail purporting to be from his widow seeking your assistance in retrieving the family's hidden money. From the telltale signs of poor grammar to the outrageous, too-good-to-be-true offer, always ask yourself why you are being selected for this great opportunity. And then delete the e-mail.

How Do Identity Thieves Steal Your Passwords?

Many of the identity theft schemes on social media involve people trusting messages and postings from their friends; however, often these messages and postings might appear to be from your friends, but actually are from identity thieves who have hacked into your friends' accounts and are sending you messages and postings that can lead to your identity theft.

Phishing or misdirecting you to a website that you think is legitimate, but is not, is one of the primary ways that identity thieves get people to input their personal information that can provide access to Facebook accounts.

Unwittingly clicking on a link that downloads a keystroke-logging malware program onto your computer is another way that identity thieves steal your passwords, as well as everything else in your computer.

It is relatively easy to get a person's e-mail address. After an identity thief has this information, the thief can then go to your e-mail account and indicate that he or she has forgotten the password and then by answering a security question, get access to your e-mail. The identity thief can then also contact Facebook from your e-mail address to change your password on Facebook and get access to your account. With so much personal information online, many people use security questions for which the answer can be found with some diligent searching. This is how Sarah Palin got her e-mail account hacked, when the hacker answered the security question as to where she met her husband, which the hacker was able to find on Wikipedia.

Identity thief Iain Wood stole $57,000 from his neighbors' bank accounts by stealing their identities through gathering information from their Facebook accounts and other social network sites that provided birthdays, mother's maiden names, and other personal information that his neighbors provided online but also used as answers to their security questions for their online banking.

Twitter

Twitter is among the social media websites that will let you use an open API by which you can log in with your Twitter password and connect with your other accounts. This makes it easy for you to tweet stories from your smartphone or other mobile devices to different accounts without having to use multiple passwords. Unfortunately, so can an identity thief, if he or she steals your password.

TIP

Give up the convenience for security. Use multiple and complex passwords.

Twitter Hacking

A common technique used by scammers and identity thieves is to send you an e-mail or a text message purporting to be from companies with which many people do business, such as large national banks, Facebook, Twitter, or eBay, telling you that there has been a security breach of your account and that it is necessary for you to take particular steps to protect your data and your account. The e-mail or text then requires you to provide confirming personal information, which then is used by the identity thief to make you a victim of identity theft, or it requires you to click on a link to take you to a page where you will be assisted in protecting your account when in actuality what you do by clicking on the link is download keystroke-logging malware that will steal all the information on your computer. A similar e-mail that many Twitter users actually received in 2012 was legitimate; however, there is more to the story. The legitimate e-mail from Twitter read "Twitter believes that your account might have been compromised by a website or service not associated with Twitter. We've reset your password to prevent others from accessing your account." The e-mail then instructed people as to how they could change their passwords to the password they now wanted to use. The number of Twitter users receiving the e-mail actually was more than the number of Twitter users who were in danger of having their accounts hijacked, but Twitter decided to err on the side of caution and change more account passwords than might have been necessary. It is hard to criticize that decision, although it is possible that the broad resetting of passwords might also have represented a mere mistake by Twitter in determining what accounts were in jeopardy. But there is another scam of which you should be aware. Knowing that the word was getting out that the e-mail from Twitter was legitimate, scammers e-mailed and texted their phony versions of this e-mail representing themselves as Twitter. In the scammers' e-mails they either asked for personal information or directed people to link to a page to reset their password that downloaded that keystroke-logging malware program I warned you about. Don't provide such information and don't click on any links unless you are sure they are legitimate.

When Target had its massive data breach in 2013, it contacted its customers, including me, informing us of the availability of credit monitoring. There was a link in the e-mail to sign up for a free credit-monitoring service. Although the e-mail I received was legitimate, it was not worth taking the risk of clicking on a tainted link, so I merely went directly to Target's website where I was able to sign up for the credit monitoring without concerns about identity theft.

Another Twitter Scam

In this scam you receive a tweet that tells you that if you click on the link contained in the tweet you will see a photograph of yourself. Unfortunately, if you click on the tweet, you don't get a photograph of yourself, but you do download a Blackhole Exploit Kit that can do any number of malicious things to you and your computer. It has keystroke-logging capabilities, so it can read the information on your computer and get access to your credit card numbers and other personal information that might be on your computer. It also can take over your computer and turn it into a zombie computer as part of a botnet by which the scammers use your computer to send out their scam e-mails.

Pinterest

Pinterest lets people share or "pin" images of their business logos, business coupons, and discounts for marketing purposes to a virtual bulletin board. Viewers can then indicate that they like the image, comment on the image, or repin it to their own boards. Identity thieves have used phony postings to get people to provide information used to make them victims of identity theft.

Tips for Safe Use of Social Networking

Following a few simple rules while using social media can help protect you from the risk of identity theft. Here are a few steps to take:

- Don't click on links from people you don't know. Those links can download keystroke-logging malware onto your computer that can steal all the personal information from your computer and make you a victim of identity theft.

- Don't click on links from people you do know. First, the sender might not be the person you know, but rather an identity thief who has hacked the Facebook account of your friend, which is quite easy to do. Second, your friend might unwittingly be passing something on to you that is loaded with malware.

- Adjust the privacy settings on your social networking sites to make it more difficult for people you don't know to post material on your page.

- Go to your social media only directly through its website. Every time you go to it through an e-mail link or another website, you risk being lured into providing your information to a phony website rather than the true social media site you are seeking.

- Don't befriend everyone. Identity thieves will contact you with phony profiles to lure you into providing information they can use to make you a victim of identity theft.

- Check out and understand the privacy policy of the various social networking sites you use. They might be providing more information than you want to share with others.

- Be careful about the apps that you download to your personal page. Free game apps are particularly dangerous sources of keystroke-logging malware. Always carefully evaluate any apps before you download them.

- If you find a link to a video on your wall that intrigues you, go to a legitimate site such as YouTube where you can find the video, if it exists, without the risks of malware and identity theft.

- Always be wary of any e-mail purporting to be from any social networking site you use that asks you to update your information.

- For some reason, many identity thieves did not pay attention in English class. Additionally, many identity theft schemes originate in foreign countries. In either instance, there is an inordinate amount of poor grammar in many identity theft scheme communications. Always be extra skeptical of an e-mail or message you get purportedly from a social networking site you use that has poor grammar or spelling.

- Make sure you are using the most up-to-date version of your Internet browser because newer versions often contain phishing protection.

- Make sure that your computer's security software is up-to-date. It is best to subscribe to a security software service that automatically updates your software.

- Do not use apps that do not use "https" at the beginning of the Web address or URL. That extra "s" means that the data is encrypted.

- If you need to access your Facebook account from a public venue, such as a library computer, you can get a one-time password that is provided by Facebook and is valid for only 20 minutes. This can help protect your privacy if that computer is hacked.

15

Steve's Rules

Following these rules can help you protect yourself from identity theft. The rules also will tell you what to do if you do become a victim of identity theft. These are my rules, some of which I even follow.

Identity Theft Protection Rules

Although this list of rules is quite lengthy, in fact, they are not particularly difficult to follow, and, by doing so, you can go a long way toward protecting yourself from becoming a victim of identity theft:

- Never give personal information over the phone to anyone whom you have not called, and always be sure of to whom you are speaking.
- Carry only the credit cards that you need to use in your wallet.
- Never carry your Social Security card in your wallet. Where is that thing anyhow?
- If you rent a car, destroy your copy of the rental agreement when you return the car.
- Consider using a post office box rather than having mail delivered to your home.
- If you don't use a post office box, use a locked mailbox at your home.
- Do not bring your checkbook with you on vacation. Use traveler's checks or credit cards.
- Keep copies of all your credit cards, front and back, as well as the telephone numbers for customer service.
- Remove yourself from marketing lists for preapproved credit cards. If you receive preapproved credit card applications that you do not use, shred them.
- Sign up for the National Do Not Call List.

- Check your credit report at least once a year. Because you can get a free copy of your credit report annually from each of the three major credit-reporting bureaus, stagger your requests so that you get one report every four months.
- Check your Social Security Statement provided by the Social Security Administration annually.
- When you get a new credit card, sign it immediately and call to activate it.
- As much as possible, keep your credit card in sight when you make a purchase to prevent it from being "skimmed."
- Check your bank statements, telephone bills, credit card statements, and brokerage account statements monthly for unauthorized charges.
- Do not download files from people you do not know, and be wary of links that might contain malware even if they come in e-mails from friends, because your friend's e-mail might have been hacked or your friend might unwittingly be sending you tainted e-mail with malware.
- Shred, shred, and shred all unnecessary financial records and preapproved credit card offers.
- Do not store your personal information on a laptop computer.
- Use antivirus software on all your electronic devices and update it regularly.
- Set up a firewall on your computer and other electronic devices.
- Remove all personal information from your hard drive when you get rid of your computer, laptop, smartphone, or other electronic devices.
- Ask any business that has your personal information about their policy for the protection of that information.
- Do not use your Social Security number as your driver's license number or on your health insurance card.
- Do not store on your computer the passwords to frequently visited websites. Enter them every time you go to the website.
- Lock your car and don't leave anything in it that you cannot risk losing.
- Store your records that contain personal information that could be used to make you a victim of identity theft in a locked, secure place.
- After you have received a loan, a credit card, or anything else that required you to complete an application containing your Social Security number, request that your Social Security number be removed from the application on record.
- When doing any financial transactions on your computer, laptop, or smartphone, make sure that your communications are encrypted.

- Don't share your passwords with anyone, and make sure you use complicated passwords that are not easily guessed. Although many people do so, your pet's name is not a good password.

- Limit the information you share on social networking sites in order to make the work of identity thieves more difficult in regard to getting your personal information.

- Read the privacy policies of any website to which you would provide personal information to find out with whom they share information and how they keep your information secure.

- Avoid privately owned ATMs.

- Always check an ATM before you use it for evidence of tampering or the installation of a skimmer. Also look for hidden cameras.

- When ordering new paper checks, don't have them mailed to your home. Pick them up at the bank.

- Don't use public copy machines for the copying of your documents that contain personal information such as your Social Security number.

- Update your laptop before going on any trip where you will be taking your laptop so that you will not be tempted by infected Internet systems in hotels that might tell you that you need to update your software.

- When making gifts to charities, don't provide your Social Security number. They do not need it and it could turn up in publicly available forms.

- When writing an obituary for a family member, do not include too much information that can be used by identity thieves.

- Pay your bills online. It is safer than sending paper checks through the mail. Just make sure that the bank's website is secure and your computer's security software is updated. If you must mail paper checks, mail them directly from the post office.

- Put a credit freeze on your credit report at each of the three credit-reporting agencies.

- If you are in the military and are deployed away from home, put an active duty alert on your credit reports at each of the three credit-reporting agencies.

- When using Wi-Fi, make sure that your wireless router has an encryption mechanism. Make sure that it is turned on.

- Use complex passwords with combinations of letters and symbols, and use different passwords for each of your accounts.

- File your income tax return early in order to avoid tax identity theft.

- Never download tax software contained in an e-mail.

- If you use a professional tax preparer, make sure that they are legitimate and that they protect your personal data.

- If you e-file your income tax return, use a strong password and store the information on a CD or flash drive in a secure place rather than on your computer's hard drive.

- If you file your income tax return by mail, do it from the post office and not a mailbox.

- Opt out of information sharing when you receive notices from companies pursuant to the Gramm-Leach-Bliley Act.

- Carefully evaluate your privacy settings on your social network sites and set them up at a level with which you are comfortable.

- Use the Do Not Track option available in your Internet browser.

- Set a security lockout on your smartphone when it is not in use.

- Go to your social media only directly through its website.

- Don't befriend everyone who asks.

- Check out the privacy policy of the various social networks you use.

- Always investigate the legitimacy of an app before you install it.

- Due to the risk that a bank, brokerage house, or other place that holds your assets might be hacked and your records lost, make backup records of all of your online accounts, and keep them on a thumb drive that you store in a locked, safe place in your home.

- Get two computers. Use one computer exclusively for online banking, purchases, and the storage of personal information. Have another computer for the children to use or for your own use that is not related to your personal finances. In this way, you avoid the risk of having someone unwittingly download a keystroke-logging malware program to steal your personal information.

- Register with your credit card issuer to receive a text message or an e-mail alert for charges to your card over an amount that you determine and in the event of any change of personal information, such as a change of address.

- Keep up-to-date with the latest news regarding identity theft by following Steve Weisman's website/blog, www.scamicide.com, which updates identity theft and scam news daily.

Rules to Follow If You Are a Victim of Identity Theft

Cognizant of Murphy's Law that what can go wrong will go wrong, you might have followed all my rules for protecting yourself from becoming a victim of identity theft and still find yourself a victim because, as I explained earlier, your personal information might be in the data banks of companies and governmental agencies that might not do a good job of protecting your information. In that instance, here are some rules to follow:

- Notify the credit-reporting agencies and have a fraud alert and a credit freeze placed on your account with each agency.

- Report the crime to the appropriate law enforcement authorities where you live and where the fraud occurred. Use the FTC's ID Theft Affidavit.

- Inform all your creditors that you have become a victim of identity theft.

- Get new credit cards with new account numbers for all tainted accounts.

- Set up passwords for new accounts.

- Change your PIN numbers (I know that this is redundant because PIN is an acronym for Personal Identification Number, but it just sounds right).

- When you close tainted accounts, make sure that the accounts are reported to the credit-reporting agencies as being closed at the customer's request due to identity theft.

- Ask your creditors to notify each of the credit-reporting agencies to remove erroneous and fraudulent information from your file.

- If your checks are stolen, promptly notify your bank and close the account immediately.

- Notify the check verification companies and request that they contact retailers that use their services to advise them not to accept checks from any checking accounts of yours that have been accessed by identity thieves.

- Contact the creditors who have tainted accounts in your name and request that they initiate a fraud investigation. Get a copy of the completed investigation.

- Send copies of those completed investigations to each of the credit-reporting agencies and request that erroneous and fraudulent information be removed from your files.

- If fraudulent charges do manage to appear on your credit report, notify the credit-reporting agencies in writing and tell them that you dispute the information, and request that such information be removed from your files.

- If you are contacted by a debt collector attempting to collect on a debt incurred by an identity thief, inform the debt collector that the debt is not yours and that you are a victim of identity theft.

- If your passport is lost or stolen, contact the State Department to report it lost or stolen and to get a new passport.

- If you are a victim of criminal identity theft, contact the police and local District Attorney's office to clear your name. Get a letter from the District Attorney explaining that you have been a victim of criminal identity theft, and carry it with you at all times.

- Be aware of identity thieves who will take advantage of the information they have gained about you to contact you under the guise of assisting you in fixing your identity theft.

16

Steve's Top Ten Lists

avid Letterman is famous for his top ten lists. I have my own top ten lists for various aspects of identity theft, and although they might not be as amusing as David Letterman's lists, they are important for you to know.

Steve's Top Ten Things the Government Should Be Doing About Identity Theft

1. The government should eliminate the use of the Social Security number as an identifying number everywhere except for Social Security itself. Although there will be initial costs involved in this process, particularly as it relates to Medicare and the income tax, it will save much money and distress in the long run as a more secure and less vulnerable identifying number is used.

2. The federal government should be taking the lead in the development of biometric identifiers.

3. Congress should enact and enforce uniform rules that both business and government should be required to follow to protect data better, such as the requirement of the encryption of all personal information data.

4. The government should require that employers file W-2s with the IRS at the same time that they are required to be filed with the Social Security Administration and cross-check these W-2s with those used in individual income tax returns before sending a refund in order to reduce income tax identity theft.

5. The government should amend the Gramm-Leach-Bliley Act to provide for consumer's personal information to be shared only among companies for which the consumer affirmatively agrees to the sharing.

6. The government should enact federal laws to protect medical records, both digital and nondigital. It should amend HIPAA to make it easier for victims of medical identity theft to remove erroneous information from their medical reports.

7. The government should enact federal law pertaining to Identity Theft Passports for the protection of victims of criminal identity theft.

8. The government should enact federal regulations requiring greater responsibility of the credit-reporting bureaus to more promptly correct errors in credit reports resulting from identity theft.

9. The government should enact federal regulations to permit freezing of the credit reports of children.

10. The government should amend the laws pertaining to debit card liability in the event of identity theft to make them the same as laws pertaining to credit card liability in the event of identity theft.

Steve's Top Ten Things Business Should Be Doing About Identity Theft

1. Business should better protect the stock exchanges, including NASDAQ, the New York Stock Exchange, banks, and other financial institutions, from hacking. These important financial institutions are vulnerable.

2. Business should develop biometric identifiers such as fingerprints, voice recognition, and handprints for increased security against identity theft.

3. Business should update credit and debit card technology to the most advanced EMV technology on an expedited basis.

4. Businesses that have no need for a person's Social Security number should cease using this as an identifier.

5. Businesses should stop retaining personal information that they do not need.

6. Businesses should do a better job of limiting their employees' access to sensitive information.

7. Business should place security as a higher priority in the development of new technologies.

8. Business should include security software in the products manufactured in the new Internet of things.

9. Business should pay greater attention to security when disposing of documents.

10. Businesses should make a greater commitment to protecting and respecting the privacy of their customers.

Steve's Top Ten Trends for the Future of Identity Theft

1. Efforts by identity thieves will be increasingly focused on smartphones and other portable devices where the perfect storm exists for identity theft—people storing sensitive personal information while failing to take the steps necessary for greater security while using these devices.

2. Data breaches in which consumer data such as credit card numbers, debit card numbers, Social Security numbers, and other personal information is stolen and used by identity thieves will increase in frequency.

3. Hackers will increasingly focus their attention on small retail businesses that compile much personal information, but too often neglect to take the proper security precautions to protect this data.

4. Organized crime will become more involved in identity theft in general and in data breaches in particular.

5. Identity theft will become more and more a transnational crime committed by organized crime based in countries around the world.

6. Identity thieves will be increasing their targeting of social media both to gather personal information to be used for identity theft and to perpetrate identity theft schemes.

7. The black markets for data sold in large data breaches will increase in number and sophistication.

8. Keystroke-logging malware will increasingly be inserted into online ads that infect your computer when you click on the ad.

9. Income tax identity theft will continue to get worse before it gets better.

10. Spearphishing will substantially increase in frequency.

Steve's Top Ten Things People Should Do to Protect Themselves from Identity Theft

1. Install proper firewalls as well as antivirus and anti-malware software on all of your electronic devices, including your computer, laptop, smartphone, and tablet.

2. Obtain apps only from legitimate app stores.

3. Password-protect all of your electronic devices with unique and complex passwords.

4. Keep your security software current with the latest security patches.

5. Never provide personal information online through a website unless the URL begins with "https."

6. Reduce the amount of personal information that you provide on social media, including your birthday.

7. Reduce the number of places that you provide your Social Security number whenever possible.

8. Cross-shred documents that contain personal information before discarding.

9. Take advantage of the offers of banks and others to use two-factor authentication.

10. Consider using two computers at home. Limit the use of one to online banking and other financial transactions. Use the other for your e-mail and other connections to the Internet. This will help avoid your unwittingly downloading keystroke-logging malware.

Index

F

Facebook
  avoiding scams, 147-148
  celebrity videos on, 148-149
  examples of scams, 146-147
  links on, 145, 148-149
  privacy protection on, 81-83
family computer, prevention of identity
  theft, 43
Family Educational Rights Privacy Act
  (FERPA), 112
faxes, spam, 20
Fazio Mechanical, 98-99
FBI warnings about data breaches, 99-100
Federal Drivers Privacy Protection
  Act, 59
Federal Express phishing scam, 8
Federal Financial Institutions Examination Council (FFIEC), 28-29
Federal Immigration Reform Act, 59
Federal Trade Commission, 52
FERPA (Family Educational Rights Pri-
  vacy Act), 112
FFIEC (Federal Financial Institutions
  Examination Council), 28-29
files, sharing, 40-41
filing police reports, 53
firewalls, 38, 88
Ford, Cora Cadia, 75
Form 990, 34
Form 8821, 70-71
foster children, identity theft of, 113
fraud alerts on credit reports, 51-52
fraud investigations by creditors, 53
fraudulent charges, disputing, 137
future of identity theft, 163

G

G20, 11-12
Gadhafi, Moammar, 150
gaming consoles, 6-7
Gates, Bill, 16
G-Data, 88
George, J. Russell, 68
Gibson, Mel, 16
Girl Scouts, 75
Global Payments, 135
GMAC, 48
Gomez, Carlos, 67
Gonzales, Albert, 95

Google
  dorking, 102
  privacy protection on, 83
government role in prevention of identity
  theft, 161-162
Griffin, John Earl, 95
Gruttadauria, Frank, 78
guessing Social Security number, 62

H

hacked e-mail accounts, recovering
  from, 42
hackers, 6. *See also* data breaches
  of celebrity information, 16
  of Internet-connected devices, 17
  universal problem of, 93
  in Wi-Fi hotspots, 44-45
hard drives, destroying, 38
Hayek, Salma, 10
Health Insurance Portability and Accountability Act (HIPAA), 142
Heartland Payment Systems, 95, 135
Hilton, Paris, 16
HIPAA (Health Insurance Portability and
  Accountability Act), 142
Holder, Eric, 69
hotels
  data breaches at, 100
  prevention of identity theft, 32-34
hotspots, 44-45
Huerta, Regina, 71

I

ID Theft Affidavit, 52
identifier broadcasters (in wireless routers), 33, 45
identity theft
  after death
    of children, 106
    Death Master File, 105-106
    preventing, 106-107
  of children. *See* children
  consequences of, 1
  criminal identity theft. *See* criminal
    identity theft
  data breaches and. *See* data breaches
  future of, 163
  medical identity theft. *See* medical
    identity theft
  methods of
    at ATMs, 26-28
    at colleges and universities, 62